BIBLE
STORIES
ABOUT JESUS

Group

Loveland, Colorado

Wiggly, Giggly Bible Stories About Jesus

Credits

Contributing Authors: Mary Ann Craven, Cynthia A. Kenney, Jan Kershner, Lori Haynes Niles, and Liz Shockey
Editor: Beth Rowland Wolf
Senior Editor: Ivy Beckwith
Chief Creative Officer: Joani Schultz
Copy Editor: Julie Meiklejohn
Art Director: Kari K. Monson
Cover Art Director: Jeff A. Storm
Computer Graphic Artist: Nighthawk Design
Illustrator: Michael Morris
Production Manager: Peggy Naylor

Library of Congress Cataloging-in-Publication Data
Wiggly, giggly Bible stories about Jesus.
     p.   cm.
  ISBN 0-7644-2046-1 (alk. paper)
  1. Christian education of preschool children. I. Group Publishing.
BV1475.7.W54 1997
268'.432--dc21
                                      97-41216
                                       CIP

10 9 8 7 6 5 4   07 06 05 04 03 02 01 00
Printed in the United States of America.
Visit our Web site: www.grouppublishing.com

Contents

Introduction

Preschoolers are just beginning to realize that the world extends far beyond their homes and families. Each day brings a multitude of new discoveries. As a part of their new discoveries, we want children to learn the basics of faith—that God, the creator of everything they see, desires a relationship with them. That's why the preschool years are the perfect time to introduce children to Jesus and to encourage what will become a lifetime friendship between each young child in your class and the Savior of the world.

That's exactly what *Wiggly, Giggly Bible Stories About Jesus* will help you do. This book is a collection of twenty-five active stories from the life of Jesus. These stories will help children understand that Jesus came to this world a baby, just as they did, and that Jesus grew up to be kind, compassionate, and loving. They'll see that Jesus is God and that he has amazing powers to heal and to calm the wind and the waves. And they'll also come to understand that Jesus, though he is God, came to our world with a heart for service and sacrifice.

These twenty-five stories will take preschoolers through the life of Christ, from his birth to his resurrection and ascension. And best of all, these stories are designed to be age-appropriate and action-packed for wiggly young children with short attention spans. For each event from Jesus' life, you'll find four fun-filled action stories that'll have children moving, singing, laughing, and *remembering* what they're learning. This book is packed with motion songs, finger plays, action rhymes, and other great techniques for engaging young children in Bible learning.

This book is super for those times when children are too wiggly and giggly to sit still during the Bible story. And you'll also find that it's just what you need when you're teaching an extended session and you need a fresh way to tell the story or to review the story.

Enjoy using the stories in *Wiggly, Giggly Bible Stories About Jesus* to introduce the children in your class to Jesus. You'll find that children love these versions of their favorite Bible stories and will want to do them over and over. And you'll love the learning that comes when excited children have fun with Bible stories.

Jesus Is Born

Luke 2:1-40

Christmas is often associated with gift-giving. It's a great opportunity to teach children about the most wonderful gift anyone has ever been given—Jesus Christ.

These four retellings of the Christmas story will help the preschoolers in your class learn that Jesus is a very special gift who was sent to be our salvation.

Jesus Christ Is Born

Sing this song to the tune of "The Farmer in the Dell." Children will enjoy the familiar pattern and beat. Introduce one verse at a time, and sing the words while you do the motions. You may even want to explain to the children the significance each verse has in the Christmas story. For example, explain how the angels appeared to the shepherds before you sing the second verse. When the children have learned all the verses, sing the entire song.

Jesus Christ is born, Jesus Christ is born *(fold arms as if rocking a baby);*
A star shines in Bethlehem *(make a diamond shape over your head with your fingers),*
Jesus Christ is born. *(Fold arms as if rocking a baby.)*

The angels praise God, the angels praise God *(move your arms like angel wings);*
A star shines in Bethlehem *(make a diamond shape over your head with your fingers),*
The angels praise God. *(Move your arms like angel wings.)*

The shepherds go to see, the shepherds go to see *(shade your eyes with your hand as you move your head from side to side)*;
A star shines in Bethlehem *(make a diamond shape over your head with your fingers)*,
The shepherds go to see. *(Shade your eyes with your hand as you move your head from side to side.)*

The wise men travel far, the wise men travel far *(march your feet)*;
A star shines in Bethlehem *(make a diamond shape over your head with your fingers)*,
The wise men travel far. *(March your feet.)*

Our Savior, he has come; our Savior, he has come *(point up, then point down)*;
A star shines in Bethlehem *(make a diamond shape over your head with your fingers)*,
Our Savior, he has come. *(Point up, then point down.)*

Baby Jesus Goes to Sleep

In this chanting song, you will speak the first part of the leader section and half-sing or chant the quoted part of the leader section. For example, in the first section you will speak the first part and then sing or chant, "Hush, hush, little baby; go to sleep." The children sing back those words and do the actions.

You can make up your own melody for the sung sections of this activity or you can sing them to tones in the minor third, which children all over the world sing. The minor third is the same tone interval as found in the childhood song "Ring Around the Rosie."

Encourage the children to do this activity softly and reverently.

If you prefer, you can simply say the words instead of singing them.

Leader: It's late at night on the day Jesus was born. Mary holds baby Jesus and rocks him. She says, "Hush, hush, little baby; go to sleep." *(Fold arms as if rocking a baby.)*
Children: Hush, hush, little baby; go to sleep. *(Children fold arms as if rocking a baby.)*

Leader: The cows mooed softly. They said, "Moo, moo, little baby; go to sleep." *(Get down on hands and knees and moo.)*
Children: Moo, moo, little baby; go to sleep. *(Children get down on hands and knees and moo.)*

Leader: The shepherds tiptoed in. They said, "Shh, shh, little baby; go to sleep." *(Tiptoe in place and put finger on lips.)*

Children: Shh, shh, little baby; go to sleep. *(Children tiptoe in place and put fingers on lips.)*

Leader: The sheep baaed quietly. They said, "Baa, baa, little baby; go to sleep." *(Stand on hands and knees and baa.)*

Children: Baa, baa, little baby; go to sleep. *(Children stand on hands and knees and baa.)*

Leader: They all sing to Jesus. They sing, "Go to sleep, little baby; go to sleep." *(Fold arms as if rocking a baby.)*

Children: Go to sleep, little baby; go to sleep. *(Children fold arms as if rocking a baby.)*

Baby Jesus Finger Play

Children love to use their fingers to tell stories. In this finger play that emphasizes the role of angels in the Christmas story, each finger represents a different character. As you speak each verse, tap one finger, starting with your thumb and moving to your fingers. The first time through the finger play, the children simply repeat your actions.

The second time through, tap your thumb and ask, "Who is this?" The children will tap their thumbs and say, "This is an angel." Say: "That's right. This is an angel." Then recite the rest of the stanza. Continue in this manner throughout the finger play.

This is an angel. *(Tap your thumb.)*
Angels brought special news to many people.

This is Mary. *(Tap your index finger.)*
An angel told her that she would have a very special baby.

This is Joseph. *(Tap your middle finger.)*
An angel told him that he was going to be the daddy.

This is a shepherd. *(Tap your ring finger.)*
Angels told him to go and find the special baby.

And this is Jesus. *(Tap your pinkie finger.)*
He's the tiny little baby God had promised to send.

Happy birthday, Jesus! *(Wiggle all your fingers.)*

Wise Men Still Seek Him

Teach children this rhyme about the wise men and then play the game that follows. If your children enjoy music, sing the rhyme to the tune of "Twinkle, Twinkle, Little Star."

Twinkle, twinkle, little star *(hold hands above head in a diamond shape);*
Wise men followed from afar. *(Shield eyes with hand.)*
They found the boy of whom we sing *(hold out hand to indicate height of the little boy)*
And gave him gifts fit for a king. *(Extend arms as if to give a gift.)*
They fell right down and gave a nod *(kneel and bow head);*
Jesus was the promised gift from God. *(Clasp hands as if in prayer.)*

After you've learned the song, play this game. You'll need a paper star the size of your hand. Explain to the children that the wise men followed the star for a long time before they found Jesus. Have one child, the wise man, leave the room with an adult helper. Help the other children hide the star. When the wise man returns, help him or her find the star having children clap quietly for "cold" and loudly for "hot." When the star has been found, sing the song again. Play until everyone has had a turn to be the wise man.

Jesus in the Temple

Luke 2:41-52

Children are eager to grow. They enjoy measuring how much they've grown and talking about what they can do now that they're "big boys" and "big girls." Children also look forward to the new skills and freedoms that growing up will bring.

Often children only think of Jesus as a tiny baby at Christmastime or as the grown man who healed people, taught, and died for us on the cross. This grouping of activities will help children see that Jesus was a boy who grew in wisdom and stature and in favor with God and man.

Jesus in the Temple

Kids will enjoy participating in an easy drama that tells about the twelve-year-old Jesus in the Temple. Have kids stand and repeat your words and actions.

I'm Mary, Jesus' mom. *(Pretend to cradle a baby in your arms.)*

I'm Joseph, Jesus' dad. *(Stand with your hands on your hips.)*

We're taking Jesus to Jerusalem for the Passover Feast. *(Walk in place.)*

Jerusalem is so far, we have to set up camp. *(Make a pointed tent with your hands and arms.)*

It's time to get some sleep! *(Lay your head on your hands.)*

In Jerusalem, we celebrate the Passover. *(Clap your hands.)*

It's time to go back home. *(Pretend to pack things up.)*

Where is Jesus? *(Put your hand over your eyebrows, as if searching.)*

We must go back to Jerusalem and find him. *(Walk in place.)*

Jesus is in God's house, talking to the teachers. *(Make praying hands, then cup your hands around your mouth.)*

We tell him we were worried! *(Put your hands on your cheeks and shake your head back and forth.)*

Jesus explains he wanted to talk about God. *(Stretch your hands outward.)*

It's time for Jesus to go back home with his mom and dad. *(Walk in place.)*

Jesus obeys his parents, and he grows up to be wise. *(Squat, then stand up slowly with your finger to your temple.)*

Where Is Jesus?

Children will love this finger play in which they discover the missing Jesus. Have the children follow your actions.

Jesus *(hold up one finger)*
and Mary *(hold up two fingers)*
and Joseph *(hold up three fingers),*
All three,
Went to Jerusalem for the Passover Feast. *("Hop" your three fingers across the front of your body.)*
And when it was done, they packed up to go home. *(Pretend to pack your things.)*

Mary *(hold up one finger)*
and Joseph *(hold up two fingers)*
Were on the road home. They walked and they walked, but soon stopped up short. *("Walk" your two upright fingers, then stop abruptly.)*
"Someone is missing!" they began to exclaim! *(Put your hands to your cheeks.)*
Who could it be? Would you like to guess? *(Hold your hands out to your sides to question.)*

It's Jesus! Oh, no! Now, where could he be? *(Put your hands on your cheeks.)*
Mary and Joseph turned around and went back to Jerusalem. *(Turn around two fingers and "march" them back.)*
They searched in the market. *(Hold your hand to your eyebrows and look to the right.)*
They searched down the roads. *(Look to the left.)*
They searched in the stables. *(Look to the right.)*
They searched everywhere! *(Look to the left.)*

Finally they went to the Temple. *(Weave your fingers together and clasp hands like at the beginning of the rhyme "Here Is the Church.")*

Inside there were lots of people *(open up your hands and wiggle the finger "people");*

And sure enough, one of them was Jesus. *(Wiggle your thumb.)*

Jesus said, "Didn't you know I'd be in my Father's house?" *(Hold your hands out to your sides to question.)*

And then Jesus *(hold up one finger)*
and Mary *(hold up two fingers)*
and Joseph *(hold up three fingers),*
All three,
Went back home to Galilee. *("March" all three fingers.)*

Oh, No! Where Is Jesus?

Sing this fun action song to the tune of "Pop! Goes the Weasel."

They traveled to Jerusalem *(walk in place)*
To celebrate the Feast *(pretend to eat);*
But on the way home, they stopped and exclaimed *(put your hands on your hips),*
"Oh, no! Where is Jesus?" *(Put your hands on your cheeks)*

They looked way up high and they looked down low. *(Put your hands to your eyes and stand on your toes, then scrunch down low.)*
For three days, they searched for Jesus. *(Hold up three fingers.)*
Then inside the Temple *(put your hands on your hips):*
Yes! There was Jesus. *(Nod your head.)*

Hide-and-Seek Jesus

This activity engages children through a popular game—Hide-and-Seek.

Choose a volunteer to be Jesus. Tell the following story. When you get to the part about Jesus not being with Mary and Joseph, pause long enough for Jesus to hide somewhere in the room while everyone else closes their eyes. When Jesus is hidden, have the rest of the class find him. Then tell the rest of the story. Play this game until everyone has had a chance to be Jesus. By the end, everyone will be able to tell you the story.

Every year, Mary and Joseph went to Jerusalem for the Passover Feast.

When Jesus was twelve, he went with them. But at the end of the feast, Jesus didn't go home with his parents. Mary and Joseph thought Jesus was lost. *(Pause now, and let Jesus hide.)*

When his parents realized that Jesus was not with them, they returned to Jerusalem to look for him! *(Have the children look for Jesus. When Jesus has been found, gather the children together and tell the rest of the story.)*

After three days they found Jesus in God's house, listening to stories about God and asking the teachers questions.

When his parents saw him, they told Jesus they had been searching for him for three days! Jesus said: "Why were you searching for me? Didn't you know I had to be in my Father's house?"

Then Jesus went home with his parents and he obeyed them. And Jesus grew up to be wise.

Jesus Is Baptized

Matthew 3:13-17

Most children are very curious about baptism. Whether it's something that happened to them as a baby or something that will happen to them in the future, kids want to know what this celebration is all about.

Help kids learn about Jesus' baptism by using these activities.

Jesus Is Baptized Finger Play

Lead kids in the following finger play. Repeat the words and motions several times to help the children remember it.

Jesus went to John one day. *(Do a walking motion with two fingers.)*
He said, "Please baptize me!" *(Clasp your hands together.)*
"You are God's Son. Thy will be done" *(point away, point up, and cup your hands)*,
Said John, on bended knee. *(Bend your first finger.)*

Out of the water, Jesus rose *(raise one finger in the air)*,
As the heavens opened wide. *(Make a fist in the air, then slowly open it.)*
This was the Son God loved so much *(point up)*
Sent to be our loving guide. *(Hug yourself.)*

Jesus and John and the Jordan

Kids love the water! What better way to tell the story of Jesus' baptism than to let kids get a "feel" for it themselves! You will need a clean rectangular pan (or a wallpaper water tub) filled with cool, clean water. You'll also need small cups and towels to dry hands with. Gather the kids around your "river," and have them follow your actions.

We use water for lots of things. It is good to drink. *(Give each child a small paper cup and have him or her dip out some water to drink.)*

It is good for washing. *(Have the children wash their hands in the water.)*

Water is good for keeping cool on hot days, too.

There is another way we use water. In church we use water to baptize people with. When people are baptized, it shows that they want to follow God. One day, John the Baptist was baptizing people in the Jordan River. Feel how cool the river water is! *(Let the children feel the water.)*

Jesus came from Galilee to see John the Baptist at the River Jordan. Jesus said to John the Baptist, "Please baptize me."

John said: "Me, baptize you? Shouldn't you baptize me?"

Jesus told John that it would please God, so John agreed to baptize him.

John baptized Jesus in the River Jordan. Feel the water that John used to baptize Jesus. *(Let the children feel the water.)*

Suddenly the heavens opened up, and the Spirit of God came down like a dove. A voice from heaven said: "This is my Son. I love him!" Raise your hands up into the air and shake them. Feel the water as it sprays over you! Doesn't it feel good? *(Let the children put their hands into the water.)*

Let's Baptize Jesus

Kids will remember that John the Baptist baptized Jesus by participating in this simple play.

You'll need a blue sheet that covers the floor for "water" and a small container of confetti in the middle of the sheet. Have one child play John the Baptist. Tell "John" to stand "in the water." Have another child play Jesus. Have "Jesus" stand next to the sheet "on the bank." Have everyone else sit in a circle around the water. They are the "heavens." Choose one of the children in the circle to be the dove.

Have the children follow your directions while you tell the following story. You may repeat the activity several times, letting the children switch roles.

One day, John was baptizing people in the Jordan River. Jesus stood on the bank and asked, "John, will you baptize me?" *(Have Jesus ask, "John, will you baptize me?")*

John answered, "But you are Jesus; you should baptize me." *(Have John say, "But you are Jesus; you should baptize me.")*

Jesus said, "It will please God for you to baptize me." *(Have Jesus walk into the water next to John and say, "It will please God for you to baptize me.")*

Then John baptized Jesus. *(Have John baptize Jesus with the confetti.)*

Then the heavens opened up. *(Have the heavens stand up and step back five steps.)*

The Spirit of God came down like a dove, and sat on Jesus' shoulder. *(Have the dove skip into the water and put his or her hand on Jesus' shoulder.)*

And a voice from heaven said, "This is my Son. I love him." *(Have the children in the circle say: "This is my Son. I love him." Then have everyone applaud.)*

Jesus Said, "Please Baptize Me."

Kids will remember Jesus' baptism by singing this song and doing the motions to the tune of "London Bridge."

Jesus said, "Please baptize me, baptize me, baptize me."
　(Clasp your hands.)
Jesus said: "Please baptize me; won't you, John?"

John the Baptist baptized him, baptized him, baptized him.
　(Pantomime baptizing someone.)
John the Baptist baptized him—baptized Jesus!

A dove came down from heaven, heaven, heaven. *(Float your hands down, and "twinkle" your fingers.)*
A dove came down from heaven. It was the Spirit of God.

God said, "Son, I love you, love you, love you." *(Hug yourself.)*
God said, "Son, I love you. You please me well."

Jesus Is Tempted

Luke 4:1-13

Preschoolers are beginning to see that they are often faced with the choice between good and bad. This is a great time to help children understand that Jesus also faced those choices and Jesus always chose to do the right thing. Learning from Jesus' example of using Bible verses to fight temptation will help children their entire lives. It's never too early to start laying the groundwork. These activities will help children learn that Jesus overcame temptation and they can, too.

Drama in the Desert

This rhyming activity is fun to do with two groups; it works best if each group has a leader. Form two groups, and have the groups stand facing each other. Stand in the middle, and lead the unison part. Don't expect the children to say the words at first. Have the leaders say the words, and have the children follow the actions. It's a good idea to have the children switch sides for the second time through.

Unison:
Jesus went to the desert to pray (fold your hands),
And after forty nights and days (show ten fingers four times),
He was hungry and ready to eat (rub your tummy)
When the devil came by and took a seat. (Bend your knees as if you're ready to sit down.)

Group One:
The devil picked up a rock, and said (pretend to pick up a rock),

"If you are God, then make this bread." *(Point to Group Two and point to the rock.)*

Group Two:
Jesus said: "Bread is good for flesh and bone *(make muscles on the words "flesh and bone"),*
But we don't live by bread alone." *(Shake your head.)*

Group One:
Satan said, "Why don't you take the riches from all the earth?" *(Spin around once.)*

Group Two:
Jesus said, "No, I worship God and will only him serve." *(Point up and bow.)*

Group One:
Satan said: "Then jump from here, way up high. *(Jump.)*
The angels will catch you, and you won't die." *(Flap your arms like wings.)*

Group Two:
Jesus said: "I won't do what you want me to. *(Point your thumb to your chest.)*
Go away now; I'm through with you!" *(Jerk your thumb to your side to indicate "get away.")*

Tell the Devil "No!"

Sing and play this finger game to the tune of "The Eency Weency Spider." Have children make one hand do a creepy, crawly motion to show how the devil creeps around tempting people. Have them make a fist with the other hand to show how strong Jesus was in battling the devil.

The devil tried to tempt
Jesus Christ to sin. *("Creep" your hand toward your fist.)*
Jesus used God's Word,
And the devil couldn't win. *(Push the creeping hand down with your fist.)*
Satan tried and tried again *(creep hand up again),*
But Jesus made him go. *(Push your hand down with your fist.)*
We can all use God's Word *(open your hands to make a "book")*
To tell the devil "No!" *(Cup your hands around your mouth and shout "No!")*

Temptation Melodrama

Most children recognize the classic hero and villain laughs from cartoons or tapes of their favorite stories. Show children how to bellow out a sinister "Ya-ha-ha-ha-ha!" and a triumphant "Aha!" before they act out the story of the conflict between the greatest hero and the most notorious villain of all time. Have the children follow your actions during this story. When you say "the devil," they should laugh the villain laugh. When you say "Jesus," have them laugh the triumphant laugh.

After you've been through the story several times, have the children also listen for the words "God's Word." When they hear those words, they can pantomime opening a book.

Jesus *(pause)* **had been praying, and he was very hungry.** *(Pat your stomach and look hungry.)*

The devil *(pause)* **knew that Jesus was hungry and got an idea.** *(Tap your finger to your temple.)*

He said, "Why don't you just turn this rock into bread?" *(Pretend to pick up a rock and eat it.)*

But Jesus *(pause)* **said: "God's Word says that people don't live by eating bread alone. It's more important that they love God's Word."** *(Cross your arms on your chest and then open your hands as if opening a book.)*

Then the devil *(pause)* **got another idea.** *(Tap your finger to your temple.)*

He said: "Maybe you'd like all the kingdoms of the world instead. If you worship me, you can have them." *(Spread out your hands to indicate the kingdoms.)*

But Jesus *(pause)* **was strong. He said, "God's Word says to worship God and serve only him."** *(Point up.)*

Then the devil *(pause)* **got another idea.** *(Tap your finger to your temple.)*

He took Jesus *(pause)* **to the highest place in the Temple.** *(Pretend to climb.)*

And he said: "Prove that you're God's Son by jumping from this high place. If you really are God's Son, the angels will save you." *(Jump.)*

But again Jesus *(pause)* **said, "God's Word says that it is not right to test God."** *(Shake your head and wag your finger.)*

And the devil *(pause)* **said: "Rats! Foiled again!" And he went away.** *(Pump your arms as if running away.)*

He's Gotta Go

This activity will help children learn that they can say no to temptation just like Jesus did. Have the children follow your actions during this fun action poem.

Whenever the devil is bothering you *(tap a friend's shoulder),*
You can do what Jesus did. *(Point up.)*
Look at the devil *(make "binoculars" with your hands),*
And tell him "No! *(Shout the word 'No!')*
God's Word says *(open a 'book' with your hands)*
Your lies aren't so! *(Pretend to push away lies.)*
Go away now *(point with your thumb to indicate 'Get out of here');*
You're bothering me. *(Cross your arms on your chest.)*
A friend of God's *(clasp your hands)*
Is what I'll be." *(Point to yourself with your thumb.)*

Jesus Chooses His Disciples

Luke 5:1-11

At the beginning of his ministry, Jesus called his disciples to follow him and learn his ways. Today, Jesus still calls disciples. Even the young children in your class can learn what it means to follow and obey Jesus. These four activities will help them learn how Jesus called twelve men to be his special friends.

Fisherman Peter

It's never dull around Peter! Let this poem, with its actions and rhythms, help introduce this colorful disciple.

Three hungry fishermen went out to sea *(hold up three fingers)*
To catch some fish for their families. *(Pretend to scoop up fish.)*
No fish in their net *(hold out empty hands to one side)*,
No fish in the sea *(wiggle fingers to the other side)*,
No fish at all for their families. *(Shrug shoulders with palms up.)*

So they pulled in their nets *(do a hand-over-hand pulling motion)*
And headed back to shore. *(Pretend to row boat.)*
They washed all their nets. *(Scrub fists together.)*
Oh, what a chore! *(Hold head with hands and shake head.)*

Then Jesus came and said to Peter *(march in place)*,
"Try taking your boat where the water is deeper." *(Point to a spot far away.)*
So fisherman Peter rowed to that spot. *(Pretend to row.)*
Now, what do you think Peter caught? *(Extend palms.)*

Fish of all shapes and fish of all sizes. *(Move arms in a gathering motion.)*

22

Hundreds and hundreds of fishy surprises! *(Put palms together and wiggle hands like a fish.)*

They filled up the boat from bottom to top. *(Do a hand-over-hand stacking motion.)*

There were so many fish that Peter had to stop. *(Hold hand in the "stop" position.)*

Jesus said, "It's fun to catch fish in the sea *(pretend to cast a fishing pole),*

But I want you to follow me." *(Do a beckoning motion.)*

Peter followed Jesus with a great big grin *("draw" a grin on your face),*

And from then on, he fished for men. *(Pretend to cast a fishing pole.)*

Peter, James, and John Follow Jesus

Teach this action song to the children by first teaching them the actions. Have them follow your actions while you sing. Then teach them the words, one line at a time. Sing the song to the tune "The Eency Weency Spider."

Peter, James, and John went out to catch some fish. *(Pretend to row a boat.)*

They fished and fished all night, but not a fish was caught. *(Pretend to cast a net.)*

So they pulled in the nets, and they turned the boat around. *(Pretend to pull the nets back in.)*

When they got back to the shore, Jesus climbed aboard the boat. *(Pretend to climb.)*

Jesus said to Peter, "If you want to catch some fish *(wag your finger),*

Row out a little farther where the water's deep and clear." *(Point to a spot far away.)*

Peter rowed the boat and they cast out all the nets *("row" the boat and "cast" the nets),*

And they caught so many fish that the nets began to break. *(Pretend to carry a heavy load.)*

Peter, James, and John were surprised at what they saw. *(Put hands on cheeks.)*

Never in their lives had they caught so many fish. *(Shake head "no.")*

That's when Jesus said, "Come on and follow me." *(Beckon with arm.)*

So they left the fish and left their boats and followed him that day. *(Walk in place.)*

Come, Little Fishy, Come

Act out the story of the calling of the disciples with this fun game. On the floor, lay out a masking tape outline of a boat. Make sure that when all the children are sitting inside the boat, the boat will feel a little crowded.

Designate two or three children to be the fishermen, and have one of the fishermen be Peter. Choose one child to be Jesus. Everyone else can be fish. Have the fishermen sit inside the boat. Have Jesus stand on one side of the room. Have all the fish sit in the sea (the rest of the room).

Tell this simplified version of the story, and direct children in acting it out.

Say: **One day three fishermen went fishing.** *(Have the fishermen pretend to fish from the boat with pretend nets.)* **They fished all night, but they didn't catch anything.** *(Have the fish inch away from the boat.)* **In the morning, they headed back for shore.** *(Have the fishermen pull in their nets and pretend to row.)*

Jesus was on the beach along with many people. He got into the fishermen's boat and began to teach all the people. *(Have Jesus get into the boat and pretend to talk.)* **When he was finished, Jesus told Peter, one of the fishermen, to row the boat into deeper water and try to catch some fish.** *(Have Jesus pretend to talk to Peter.)* **Peter said: "Jesus, we've been fishing all night and we haven't caught even one fish. But if you say so, we'll try again."** *(Have Peter pretend to talk to Jesus. Then have the fishermen pretend to row the boat.)*

The fishermen cast their nets in the water, and when they pulled them in, there were so many fish that the boat was full from top to bottom. *(Have all the fish come and sit in the boat.)*

The fishermen were amazed at what they saw. *(Have the fishermen look surprised and put their hands on their faces.)* **Jesus said: "Come and follow me. From now on you won't catch fish. Instead you will be fishers of men—you'll help people learn to follow me."** *(Have Jesus pretend to talk to the fishermen.)* **So the fishermen left the fish and left the boat, and they followed Jesus.** *(Have the fishermen follow Jesus as he walks around the room.)*

24

This Is the Fish That Peter Caught

In this action poem, the familiar rhythm of "The House That Jack Built" will delight preschoolers. Go through the verses and motions slowly. There's no need to rush. Let the children relax and enjoy the rhythm. By the time you've gone through all the verses, the children will be anticipating your words and your actions.

This is the fish that Peter caught. *(Measure a "fish" with your hands.)*

This is the net *(make a circle with your arms)*
That found the fish that Peter caught. *(Measure a fish with your hands.)*

This is the boat *(pretend to row a boat)*
That carried the net *(make a circle with your hands)*
That found the fish that Peter caught. *(Measure a fish with your hands.)*

These are the men *(hold up three fingers)*
Who rowed the boat *(row a boat)*
That carried the net *(make a circle with your arms)*
That found the fish that Peter caught. *(Measure the fish.)*

This is the Savior, Jesus *(point up),*
Who directed the men *(hold up three fingers)*
Who rowed the boat *(row a boat)*
That carried the net *(make a circle with your arms)*
That found the fish that Peter caught. *(Measure the fish.)*

"Come follow me" *(beckon with your arms),*
Said the Savior, Jesus *(point up),*
Who directed the men *(hold up three fingers)*
Who rowed the boat *(row a boat)*
That carried the net *(make a circle with your arms)*
That found the fish that Peter caught. *(Measure the fish.)*

And here they go. *(March in place.)*

The Woman at the Well

John 4:1-30

This story teaches a wonderful lesson—that Jesus loves everyone no matter who they are or what they've done. Jesus truly does offer each one of us living water. This water completely satisfies our thirst and brings us eternal life.

Use these activities to help children know that Jesus loves and accepts them just as he loved and accepted the Samaritan woman at the well.

God's Love Is for Everyone

Teacher Tip

Preschoolers may have difficulty understanding the concept of living water—they may think that Jesus had magic water that people could actually drink. Explain that when Jesus said he had living water, he meant that he had a special gift that would make people happy forever. Tell the children that the special gift is eternal life. We receive Jesus' special gift when we believe him and put our trust in him.

Children love to dance and sing. Teach them simple movements to go with this song that tells the story of the woman at the well. Have everyone stand in a circle and hold hands. On the first line, walk to the right. On the second line, walk to the left. On the third line, lift your hands high, and clap to the beat on the fourth line. Sing the song to the tune of "The Farmer in the Dell."

"I am thirsty, ma'am.
I am thirsty, ma'am.
I'd like a drink of water, please,"
Said Jesus at the well.

"You've been kind to me.
You've been kind to me,
Although I am a Samaritan,"
Said the woman at the well.

"You must be the Christ.
You must be the Christ.
You know all things that I have done,"
Said the woman at the well.

The woman at the well,
The woman at the well,
"Jesus loves everyone,"
Said the woman at the well.

The Well

During this story, children will drink from Jacob's well as Jesus did during the story of the woman at the well.

Set up a large bucket of clean, drinkable water. If you'd like, you can decorate it with poster board to look like a well. You'll also need small cups.

Tell this story, and have children enjoy dipping out a cup of water at the prompt.

One day Jesus was traveling along a hot, dusty road. At noon, he stopped at Jacob's well in the land of Samaria. He was very thirsty.

Along came a Samaritan woman. She had a jug with her that she wanted to fill with water from the well. Jesus asked her, "Please may I have a drink of water?" *(Have the children each dip out a cup of water and drink it.)*

The woman said: "But you are Jewish. Why are you even speaking to me? Who are you? Don't you know that Jewish people don't like Samaritans?"

But Jesus said: "If you knew who I was, you'd want what I have. I can give you eternal life."

The woman said, "I'd like that."

Jesus said, "Go get your husband and bring him here."

The woman replied, "But I don't have a husband."

Jesus said: "That's right. You are telling the truth."

The woman was amazed that Jesus knew everything about her. She said, "You must be a prophet."

Jesus said, "I am the Messiah, God's Son."

Then the woman hurried back to town. She was in such a hurry that she left her water jug at the well. She told everyone she knew about Jesus.

The Woman's Story

Rhyming stories are always fun. This one is told from the perspective of the woman who met Jesus at the well. Young children love rhythm, so exaggerate the singsong feel of this story while the children follow your actions.

Listen to me, I've a story to tell. *(Cup your ear with your hand.)*
It happened at noon when I went to the well. *(Point to an imaginary watch.)*

At the well was a man. He was Jewish, no doubt. *(Raise your hand to show the height of the man.)*
"I'll bet he's not nice," I said with a pout. *(Cross your arms on your chest.)*

The man said to me, "Please get me a drink." *(Clasp your hands together.)*
His smile was so warm that my cheeks turned quite pink. *(Put your hands to your cheeks.)*

"The Jews that I know are not nice to Samaritans. *(Frown and shake your head.)*
Since you're talking to me, you can't be just anyone." *(Shrug your shoulders.)*

He smiled and he said: "If you knew who I was *(wag your finger),*
You'd want some of my living water because *(pretend to drink)*

The water I have doesn't come from a spring. *(Shake your head.)*
But it's pure and it's good. New life it will bring. *(Rub your tummy.)*

Now go get your husband and bring him back here. *(Make a motion as if to shoo away.)*
Hurry right back. Do not disappear." *(Beckon with your hand.)*

"But sir," then I said, "I don't have a husband." *(Shrug your shoulders.)*
But he knew the truth. He knew all that I'd done. *(Put your hands on your hips.)*

"You must be a prophet," I said with a nod. *(Nod your head.)*
But he said that he was the promised Son of God. *(Point up.)*

That's when I left him and came straight to you *(pretend to run)*

To spread all my joy and to tell you the news. *(Extend your arms to indicate spreading joy.)*

He must be the Christ. Our love he'll receive *(nod your head and hug yourself)*

When we hear the truth and decide to believe. *(Cup your hand to your ear, then press your hands to your heart.)*

The Woman at the Well

Help kids realize that Jesus' love is for everyone by asking them to participate in this drama. Have kids stand and repeat your actions while you say the words.

One day, Jesus was traveling to a place called Galilee. *(Walk in place.)*

When he got tired, Jesus passed by a Samaritan city and decided to sit by a well and rest. *(Sit down and put your head on your hands.)*

A Samaritan woman saw Jesus when she came to draw some water out of the well. *(Pretend to pull water out of a well.)*

Jesus said to the woman, "I would like a drink!" *(Pretend to drink from a cup.)*

The Samaritan woman said: "Why are you talking to me? Jewish people don't even speak to people from Samaria." *(Raise your hands as if to ask a question.)*

Jesus said to her, "If you knew who I really am, you would ask *me* for a glass of water and I would give you special *living* water." *(Pretend to drink from a cup.)*

The Samaritan woman didn't understand. She asked: "How could you give me water? You don't have a bucket, and the well is very deep!" *(Pretend to peer down the well.)*

Jesus said: "The water from this well is regular water. If you drink it, you'll get thirsty again. But the water I have will bubble up like a fountain of eternal life—you'll never be thirsty again."

The Samaritan woman liked the sound of that! *(Clap your hands.)*

She said, "Sir, please give me some of this water so that I will never be thirsty again!" *(Shake your head.)*

Then Jesus told her to go get her husband and come back to the well. *(Point away from yourself, then beckon with your hand.)*

The woman said she wasn't married, and Jesus said that she was honest. *(Shake your head "no," then smile.)*

The woman said, "You must be a prophet because you knew I wasn't married even before I told you." Jesus told the woman that he was the Messiah, the Son of God. *(Make a cross in the air.)*

Then the Samaritan woman went to the city to tell everyone what had happened. *(Run in place with your hands beside your mouth.)*

Jesus Heals a Lame Man
Luke 5:17-26

The Bible tells us that Jesus performed many miracles. The story of Jesus healing the lame man who was let down through the roof emphasizes not only Jesus' compassion and power, it also gives us a glimpse into friendship and faith.

Have fun using the following activities any time you want to teach your children about Jesus, his miracles, faith, or friendship.

Friends Helping Friends Rhyme

Children will enjoy learning this fun action rhyme about friends. Have children form pairs and face their partners. You may want to choose a child to be your partner as you teach children the rhyme and motions. Repeat the rhyme several times so children can learn the words and actions.

Once there was a man who couldn't walk.
  (Pat your legs.)
As he sat on his mat, he heard people talk.
  (Cup your hand to your ear.)
"Jesus is here! Quick, come see!" *(Motion to come along.)*
The poor man said, "Hey, what about me?"
  (Point to yourself.)

Just that minute, his friends came by. *(Partners wave to each other.)*
"Don't worry, pal; we won't pass you by." *(Partners pat each other's shoulders.)*

Teacher Tip

Be sensitive to any children in your class with disabilities. A disabled child may wonder why Jesus healed the lame man but hasn't healed him or her. Explain that Jesus loves each of us and has a special plan for each of our lives. You may want to have your pastor address the class on this subject.

Then they picked him up, with his mat and all *(partners pretend to lift their friend together),*
And carried him high—boy, he sure felt tall! *(Partners walk in place, holding their friend high.)*

They got to the house where Jesus taught. *(Partners pretend to set their friend down.)*
There were so many people—lots and lots! *(Stand on tiptoe, trying to see.)*
They climbed to the roof and made a hole in the tiles. *(Pretend to climb, then make a digging motion.)*
They lowered the man. He arrived in style! *(Partners pretend to lower their friend.)*

Jesus said to the man on the mat *(pretend to look down at a man on the floor),*
"Stand up and walk." And that was that! *(Partners shake hands.)*
The man stood up and sang God's praise *(cup your hands around your mouth),*
And he served the Lord for the rest of his days. *(Clap your hands.)*

Stand-Up Song

Children will enjoy learning this song about the paralyzed man Jesus healed. Sing the song any time you want to remind your class that Jesus can do anything! Sing the words to the tune of "Jesus Loves Me."

Have the children sit in a circle with their legs crossed. They should sit close enough together so that they can pat their neighbors' knees or backs on the third line of the song. Also, have the children sit as they sing most of the words, but have them stand when they sing the words "stand up."

Once there was a man so blue. *(Tug down at the corners of your mouth.)*
He couldn't walk like me or you. *(Shake your head "no.")*
Friends helped him the Lord to meet. *(Pat your friends on the back or the knee.)*
Jesus said, "Stand on your feet." *(Stand the first two fingers of one hand on the palm of your other hand.)*

"Stand up," Jesus said. *(Stand up, then sit.)*
"Stand up," Jesus said. *(Stand up, then sit.)*

"Stand up," Jesus said. *(Stand up, then sit.)*
"Your faith has made you well." *(Extend your hands.)*

The Man and the Mat Game

We all know that young children have lots of energy, and this game takes that simple fact into account. Play this game when you teach about how Jesus healed the lame man or any time you discuss Jesus' miracles.

Have children stand on one side of the room and form pairs. Give each pair a construction paper "mat." Have partners stand facing each other, holding their mat between them. Tell children to balance the mat between them, touching it with only two fingers.

Ask children to listen carefully as you tell the Bible story. Each time they hear the word "mat," partners should walk to the opposite side of the room, balancing their mat between them. If a mat falls to the ground, just have the pair pick it up and resume walking.

Read the following story, pausing to give children time to travel with their mats.

One day, Jesus was teaching lots of people. In the crowd was a man who couldn't walk. He was sitting on a mat. *Pause.*

The man's friends wanted to help him meet Jesus. So they picked up the man and his mat *(pause),* and they carried him to the house where Jesus was teaching. But there were so many people, they couldn't get their friend anywhere near Jesus.

So they set the man down on his mat *(pause)* while they thought about what to do.

"I know!" said one of the friends. "We'll go in through the roof."

So they picked up the man and his mat *(pause)* and slowly began to climb to the roof. They climbed and they climbed, and they were very careful not to let go of the mat. *Pause.*

Finally they reached the roof. They were so tired they needed a rest. So they set down the man and his mat. *Pause.* After a short while, they made a hole in the roof, and they carefully lowered down the man and his mat. *Pause.*

Jesus saw how much faith these men had in him. They believed that Jesus could make the man walk again. They knew that Jesus could do anything!

And he can!

Jesus said, "Stand up, and take up your mat." *Pause.*

And do you know what happened? The man stood right up, and he picked up his mat! *Pause.* Then the man began praising God. How wonderful it is that Jesus can do anything!

Rooftop Snack

Few things engage a preschooler's attention as quickly as the promise of a yummy snack. Your children will pay attention to this fun Bible story because they'll be listening for directions on how to make their treats.

Set out several bowls of small square cereal such as Life or Chex, bagels cut in half, peanut butter, paper plates, and plastic knives.

Have children form trios, and give each trio a small jar or bowl of peanut butter. Give each child a bagel half on a paper plate and a plastic knife.

Read the following story rhyme, and lead children in doing the motions. Children will create delicious rooftop snacks that they can enjoy after the story. (You may want to repeat the lines after children perform a lengthy task such as spreading peanut butter.)

As Jesus was teaching in a house one day *(shake your index finger),*
A sound up above made some people say *(look up and point),*
"What's on the roof? What was that noise?" *(Hold your bagel above your head.)*
"Nothing," said others. "Prob'ly just some boys." *(Lower your bagel.)*

"This roof is strong with lots of mud all over *(spread your bagel with peanut butter),*
With lots of tiles to form a cover. *(Place the cereal on the peanut butter.)*
We're safe under here, there's nothing to harm us. *(Carefully hold your bagel up.)*
Nothing's going on that could alarm us." *(Lower your bagel.)*

Little did they know that just at that minute *(pretend to look at an imaginary watch),*
Some men on the roof made a hole right in it! *(Put one finger through the hole in your bagel.)*
They lowered down a friend who couldn't walk *(wiggle the finger that's sticking through the bagel);*
I'll tell you, brother, that stopped the talk! *(Put your hand over your mouth.)*

Now, what do you think happened to that man? *(Shrug your shoulders.)*

Jesus said, "Get up, you're able to stand." *(Stand up.)*

The man stood up; his legs were like new! *(Flex your knees.)*

That's the end of the story. I'm hungry! Aren't you? *(Rub your tummy.)*

After the story, offer a quick prayer thanking Jesus for taking care of the man on the mat and for taking care of us. Then invite children to enjoy the rooftop snacks they made during the story. Be sure to have wet washcloths handy for sticky hands.

Jesus Teaches the People

Various passages

While Jesus' ministry to us was certainly one of healing and redemption, it was also one of teaching. The earthly days of Jesus were filled with lessons for the people—how we should live, how we should treat each other, and how we should relate to our Heavenly Father. Jesus taught no matter where he was. There was so much for him to teach and his time was so short that he used every opportunity of daily life to help people understand his message.

Preschoolers intuitively understand this urgency, because they, too, are compelled to use every moment for learning. Use these activities to help kids recall specific instances of Jesus' teaching ministry. These activities work any time your lesson is about Jesus' teaching. You might want to use these activities when your lesson is the Sermon on the Mount or when you teach about any of the parables.

Wiggly, Waggly

Kids will love this nonsense rhyme and will want to make up more and more verses! Help them direct their thoughts to the many events in Jesus' life. Older preschoolers may say the first line and then guess the rhyming word that tells where Jesus taught.

Wiggly, Waggly, Will (*wiggle all over, waggle as though you have a tail, then wrap forearms around each other*),
Jesus taught from a hill. (*Two claps after the line is said.*)

Wiggly, Waggly, Woat (*wiggle all over, waggle as though you have a tail, then wrap forearms around each other*),
Jesus taught from a boat. (*"Row" with your arms.*)

Wiggly, Waggly, Wemple *(wiggle all over, waggle as though you have a tail, then wrap forearms around each other),*
Jesus taught in the Temple. *(Two claps after the line is said.)*

Wiggly, Waggly, Wible *(wiggle all over, waggle as though you have a tail, then wrap forearms around each other),*
Jesus taught from the Bible. *(Make a book with your hands.)*

Wiggly, Waggly, Whoa *(wiggle all over, waggle as though you have a tail, then wrap forearms around each other),*
Jesus taught wherever he would go. *(Walk in place.)*

The People Followed Jesus

This following song is sung to the tune of "The Bear Went Over the Mountain."

Choose one child to be "Jesus." Have Jesus lead the rest of the children on a walk around the room. On the last line of the verse, the children will stop walking and the child who is leading will pantomime something Jesus taught. The others will copy the action. For example, after teaching the parable of the seeds, the leader could pantomime planting, watering, or tending. Children can also say something that Jesus taught; for example, a child who is playing the role of Jesus might say, "Be kind to others." Then all of the children would repeat, "Be kind to others." Repeat the game several times with different children as leaders.

The people followed Jesus,
The people followed Jesus,
The people followed Jesus,
And he began to teach.

Signs of His Teaching

Use this quietly beautiful story adapted from American Sign Language just before prayer time to tame the wiggles.

Jesus sometimes taught in the morning *(hold your left arm in front of you, and bend the elbow toward you at ninety degrees. Then touch the right hand to the inner elbow. Raise the right arm upward, as if your hand is the sun coming up over the horizon),*
Sometimes in the afternoon. *(Continue pivoting your right arm to the right as far as is comfortable.)*

Sometimes he taught in the evening *(position your left hand palm-down in front of your chest. Bring your right hand over the left fingertips and down behind the left wrist as though the sun is going down over the horizon)*

In a dark and crowded room. *(Form two walls of the room by using hands with palms facing each other straight out. Drop the hands an inch or two, then face both palms toward the body to make the other two walls and drop the hands in the same way.)*

He taught on high hills *(reach up with your right hand),*

He taught in towns *(clasp your fingertips together and apart several times, moving arms from side to side),*

And he even taught from a boat *(make a rowing motion)*

While waves gently rocked him *(rock from side to side)*
And kept the boat afloat. *(Continue rocking.)*

He always told the people *(hold your right index finger in front of your mouth and move it in little forward circles)*

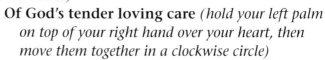
Of God's tender loving care *(hold your left palm on top of your right hand over your heart, then move them together in a clockwise circle)*

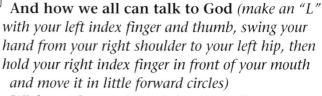
And how we all can talk to God *(make an "L" with your left index finger and thumb, swing your hand from your right shoulder to your left hip, then hold your right index finger in front of your mouth and move it in little forward circles)*

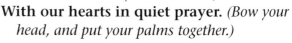
With our hearts in quiet prayer. *(Bow your head, and put your palms together.)*

Sounds Around His Teaching

Involve kids in this sound play as they review places Jesus taught.

Everywhere Jesus went, he taught people. Jesus walked from town to town with his disciples. He often taught them as they walked. *(Cup your hands and clap them against your legs in a walking rhythm.)*

Sometimes he taught at the Temple, where his sandals slapped against the cold stone floor. *(Gently slap the top of one hand and then the other.)*

Sometimes he taught in tall wheat fields where the wind brushed the grains together to make whispery music. *(Rub your palms together in circles.)*

He taught the people under trees, where the birds whistled their cheerful songs. *(Have the children try to whistle by sucking in and blowing out. When they do it all together, it should roughly approximate a few birds in the trees.)*

He taught from the middle of a quiet lake, where tiny waves lapped against the side of the boat *(have the children make smacking noises with their mouths),*

And he taught in the middle of roaring storms at sea. *(Have half the children make whooshing noises and half the children rapidly tap their feet.)*

He taught from hillsides that may have echoed back his words. *(Have the children echo back your words as you say some of the following: "Love your neighbor!" "Love God with all your heart!" "Follow me!" "Make disciples!" "Be a servant!")*

Everywhere Jesus went, he was always teaching *(review all the sounds you made in reverse order)*

...in storms...
...in quiet waters...
...under trees...
...in wheat fields...
...in the Temple...
...slowly walking with his friends...
Jesus was always, always teaching!

Whew! *(Sit down on the floor and roll to a laying position as though you are exhausted!)*

Jesus Calms a Storm

Mark 4:35-41

Preschoolers need to know that while Jesus promises to love and comfort us always, he also is stronger and more powerful than anyone. This story demonstrates the great power of our gentle Savior. And these story activities will help children know that "even the wind and the waves obey him."

Small Boat, Large Storm

Children will enjoy acting out this simple drama. Each of the parts is fun, and the children will want to take turns with the different parts.

Set up three chairs in a row, train-style. Have the children sit in a circle around the chairs. Explain to them that they will be acting out the story of Jesus calming the storm. Everyone in the circle will be the "wind" and the "waves." The wind blows (say "whoo"), and the waves splash (pat floor with hands). Have children practice.

The chairs are the "boat." Three children will sit in them and be "Jesus' special friends." They will "row" the boat. Have children practice the rowing motion. One child will be "Jesus." He will sleep in the back of the boat (behind the chairs) until it's time for him to stand and tell the wind and the waves to stop. Demonstrate what he will do. The story will tell everyone what to do. The teacher should sit with the wind and waves and lead them. Choose children for the parts and begin.

> **One day Jesus and his friends went for a ride in a boat.** *(Jesus and friends walk over to the boat.)*
> **Jesus' friends rowed** *(friends "row"),*

And Jesus went to sleep. *(Jesus "sleeps.")*
The wind gently blew. *(Wind blows gently, saying "whoo.")*
The waves gently splashed. *(Waves pat the ground gently.)*

Soon the wind started to blow stronger. *(Wind says "whoo" a little louder.)*
The waves started to splash harder. *(Waves pat the ground a little harder.)*
The friends in the boat rowed harder. *(Friends row a little harder.)*
Jesus kept sleeping. *(Jesus keeps sleeping.)*

The wind blew even stronger. *(Wind says "whoo" loudly.)*
The waves splashed even harder. *(Waves pat very hard and continue until Jesus says "stop.")*
Jesus' friends rowed harder. *(Friends row harder.)*
Jesus' friends were afraid. They yelled, "Help, help!" *(Friends yell, "Help, help!")*

Jesus stood up. *(Jesus stands up.)*
He looked at the wind and the waves and said "Stop." *(Jesus looks at the wind and the waves and says "Stop.")*
Jesus' friends looked at each other and said *(friends look at each other),*
"Who is this Jesus? Even the wind and the waves obey him."

Row, Row, Row Your Boat

In this game, the children will become boats out on the stormy sea.

Divide children into groups of two or three. Each group makes a "boat" by holding onto each others' forearms, forming a small, tight circle. The boats will move slowly around the room as you tell the story.

We're rowing our boats out to the sea.
All is gentle as can be. *(Children move boats slowly around the room.)*

Oh, no! The wind is starting to blow,
And the waves in the sea are starting to grow. *(Have children bend their knees and move their boats up and down.)*

Lord Jesus is asleep in the bow,

Let's wake him so he will help us now. *(Have children continue bending their knees and making their boats go up and down.)*

Jesus stands up and speaks to the storm,
And the wind and the waves, they blow no more. *(The boats stop moving and stay very still.)*

We're rowing our boats out to the sea;
All is gentle as can be. *(Have children move boats slowly around the room.)*

Stop, Storm, Stop

This is an extremely active game as the children actually become the storm that Jesus calms.

Beforehand, put a strip of masking tape on the floor of the classroom or outside on the playground. The masking tape should be about twelve to fifteen feet long. Three half-sheets of newspaper will be needed for each child.

Form two groups, and have one group stand on one side of the masking tape and one group on the other side. Say: **Let's play a game about the stormy sea. One day, Jesus and his disciples were sailing in a boat. Jesus was sleeping in the boat while the disciples were rowing the boat. Then a storm came up. Let's make storm noises by crumpling the newspaper in little balls. We'll pretend it's the sound of the rain.**

Have the children in each group crumple the pieces of newspaper into small balls and lay them on their side of the masking tape line.

Then say: **Now let's pretend that these balls are the raindrops that are falling in the terrible storm. We'll throw them back and forth across the line until Jesus calms the storm. While you're throwing raindrops, listen for Jesus' voice saying, "Stop." Then stop throwing raindrops.**

Signal the children to begin throwing raindrops back and forth across the tape line. Continue for a few minutes and then call out "Stop!" in a loud voice. When the children have stopped throwing raindrops, say: **The storm blew and blew, and the disciples got scared. They woke Jesus up and he said, "Be still." And immediately the wind and the waves and the rain all stopped.**

Play the game again if you'd like. The children may enjoy taking turns as Jesus.

Jesus Feeds Five Thousand People

Matthew
14:13-21

*C*hildren love to hear amazing stories. And what could be more amazing than Jesus feeding more than five thousand people with just two fish and five loaves of bread?

Use these activities to help children see that Jesus is the maker of amazing miracles! The more young children learn about Jesus with his amazing works and his amazing love, the sooner they'll come to know him as God's own Son. And that's what it's all about, isn't it?

Something to Cheer About

Use this simple cheer to involve children in the Bible story about Jesus feeding the five thousand. Repeat the cheer several times with the children until they know the words. Encourage them to hold up the number of fingers that correspond with the words. On the line "And still there was more!" have the children extend their arms wide.

> **One thousand,**
> **two thousand,**
> **three thousand,**
> **four!**
> **Five thousand fed,**
> **And *still* there was more!**

Then read the following story, and have children call out the cheer every time a number is mentioned in the story. Young children may need help identifying numbers that are spoken. For young preschoolers, pause dramatically when it's time to repeat the rhyme.

This is the story of how Jesus fed five thousand *(pause)* people with just a little bit of food.

One day Jesus and his twelve *(pause)* disciples went out to a quiet place in the country. But when the people in towns heard that Jesus was near, they went out to see him. There were lots and lots of people. How many people were there? Five thousand! *Pause.*

Jesus loved the people, and he was sad because so many were sick. Jesus healed many of them. When it got to be dinner time, a few of the twelve *(pause)* disciples said to Jesus, "It's getting late. We'd better send these people home to get something to eat."

Then Jesus answered, "They don't need to go home. We'll give them something to eat."

"But Jesus," said his disciples, "We have only five *(pause)* loaves of bread and two *(pause)* fish."

So Jesus told his followers to bring the food to him. Then he asked the people to sit down in groups. Some of the groups had fifty or a hundred *(pause)* people in them.

Then Jesus picked up the five *(pause)* loaves of bread and the two *(pause)* fish. He looked up to heaven and gave thanks to God. Then he broke the five *(pause)* loaves of bread into pieces and gave the bread to the people.

And guess what? Everyone had plenty to eat! And there was even bread left over—twelve *(pause)* baskets of bread! And that's how Jesus fed the five thousand. *Pause.*

Friendly-Fish Snacks

Children will enjoy this active snack as they learn about one of Jesus' most well-known miracles. Tell the story of Jesus feeding the five thousand as you help children make the snack. Or have your class make the snack before the story and then let children munch away as they listen.

Before this activity, gather together the following supplies: small paper plates, plastic knives, napkins, square crackers, oval crackers, small bowls of softened cream cheese, blue food coloring, small mandarin orange slices, and raisins. Before this activity, use the food coloring to tint half of the cream cheese blue. You'll need regular cream cheese and tinted cream cheese for each group.

After children have washed their hands, have them form groups of four. In each group, let children each choose one of the following roles: Fish Dishers, Super Spreaders, Fin Finders, and Steady Servers.

The Fish Dishers will spread the square crackers with blue cream cheese to make the "ocean." They'll put two crackers on each plate.

The Super Spreaders will spread white cream cheese on the oval crackers. They'll stick the oval crackers to the square crackers. Then the Fin Finders will add mandarin orange "tails." The Steady Servers will add raisin "eyes" and then they'll place the plates on the serving table.

After a simple prayer, let your children "dive in" to this tasty treat. For extra fun, provide Goldfish crackers to complete your underwater scenes.

Five-Thousand Rhyme

Rhyming stories are wonderful tools for teaching preschoolers. Children love the singsong cadence, and when you add motions to the words, the story's complete!

Five thousand people,
Sitting on a hill *(hold up five fingers),*
Listening to Jesus
To learn his will. *(Cup your hand to your ear.)*

It got quite late;
Tummies started to growl. *(Rub your tummy.)*
The disciples said,
"Let 'em eat in town." *(Wave away as if saying, "Aw, go on.")*

"No," said Jesus,
"You feed them right here." *(Point to the floor.)*
The disciples couldn't
Believe their ears. *(Pretend to shake water out of your ear.)*

"But Lord," they said,
"We don't have enough. *(Hold out your hands.)*
To feed five thousand
Would be way too tough." *(Shake your head.)*

"You know all we have
Are five loaves of bread *(hold up five fingers)*

And two little fish,"
the disciples said. *(Hold up two fingers.)*

Jesus took the food,
And after he said grace *(place your hands together in praying position)*,
An amazing thing
Happened in that place! *(Place your hands on your face as if surprised.)*

Five thousand people
Were fed in that day *(hold up five fingers)*
With lots left over!
Let's shout "hooray!" *(Clap your hands.)*

Five-Thousand Finger Play

Young children love finger plays, and this one will introduce your little ones to one of Jesus' amazing miracles. Repeat the finger play several times with your children so they can learn the words and actions.

Five thousand came to hear Jesus talk. *(Hold up five fingers.)*
They were so hungry after such a long walk. *(Walk in place.)*
"We've got no food," the disciples said. *(Hold out empty hands.)*
"Just two little fish and five loaves of bread." *(Hold up two fingers on one hand and five on the other.)*

Jesus took the food and began to pray *(fold your hands as if praying)*;
Then he broke the bread and gave it all away. *(Pretend to hand bread to a neighbor.)*
"Five thousand fed!" the disciples said *(hold up five fingers)*,
"With two little fish and five loaves of bread!" *(Hold up two fingers on one hand and five on the other.)*

46

Jesus Walks on the Water

Matthew 14:22-36

Children love a good story—and this is a great one! Children will be fascinated by the fact that Jesus was able to walk on water. And they'll be equally fascinated to see that Peter's belief enabled him to walk on the water also.

Use these activities to help kids connect this wonderful story to how they can believe in Jesus.

A Sailing Snack

Help children learn this story by using these unusual ingredients. Make blueberry finger-gelatin according to the instructions on the back of a package of gelatin. Pour the liquid gelatin into a muffin pan. After the gelatin is firm, pop it out of the muffin pan. Serve the gelatin on napkins. For each child you will need five Teddy Grahams, a muffin cup-sized portion of blueberry finger-gelatin, and a candy orange-slice. Make four slits crosswise in each orange slice.

Tell the story and have the children act it out with their snack.

Jesus told his disciples to get into the boat while he prayed. *(Give each child a piece of finger gelatin. Have each preschooler put four Teddy Grahams into the slits of his or her orange-slice boat and place the boat in the gelatin, which is the water.)*

The wind blew and blew, and the boat moved far away from the shore! *(Tell the children to imitate wind by blowing on the gelatin.)*

The next morning, Jesus came to the disciples by walking across the water! Jesus didn't sink—he walked right on top

of the water. *(Have the children take the remaining Teddy Grahams and "walk" them onto the water.)*

When Peter saw Jesus, he wanted to try it, too! Jesus said, "Peter, come to me!" *(Have the children each take a Teddy Graham out of the boat and walk it toward Jesus.)*

The wind started to blow, and Peter was afraid! *(Have the children blow on the gelatin and then push the Peter Teddy Grahams down in the gelatin.)*

"Save me!" Peter cried. And Jesus reached out his hand and helped Peter. *(Have the children lift the Peter Teddy Grahams back up onto the gelatin.)*

The disciples said, "Truly, you are the Son of God!" *(Have the children say, "You are the Son of God!")*

Enjoy eating the snack together.

The Disciples Went Out on the Water

Teach this song to the tune of "My Bonnie Lies Over the Ocean." Have the children stand up and sit down every time they sing the word "Jesus." Repeat the song several times, speeding up as you go.

**The disciples went out on the water
While Jesus stayed back, knelt, and prayed.
My Jesus then walked upon water!
When Peter decided to say,
"Jesus, Jesus, I want to walk out there with you, with you!"
"Peter, Peter, come out here and be with me, too!"**

**The wind started blowing and scared him
And then Peter started to sink.
He said, "Please, Lord, won't you save me?"
And Jesus asked, "Why do you doubt?"
Truly, truly, Jesus is God's Son for me, for me!
Truly, truly, Jesus is God's Son for me.**

Jesus Walks on the Water—A Play

Help kids to understand this story through playacting. You'll need a sheet.

Begin by spreading the sheet out on the floor. Ask everyone to squat around the sheet, holding onto the edges. As you tell the following story, ask the kids to do the activities that accompany it.

While the disciples waited for Jesus in the boat, the wind blew the boat into the waves. *(Have the children each shake their part of the sheet up and down. Watch as the sheet ripples like waves!)*

The next morning, Jesus went out to meet his disciples by walking on the water! *(Let the "water" rest calmly on the floor.)*

Peter said: "Lord! Let me come out into the water with you!" *(Ask one child to be Peter, and have him or her walk into the center of the sheet.)*

The wind began to blow, and Peter was afraid. He started to sink in the water! *(Tell the children to stand up, holding the sheet up around Peter.)*

Peter cried: "Jesus! Save me!" and Jesus reached out his hand and helped Peter. *(Tell the children to spread the sheet out flat onto the floor again.)*

The disciples said, "Truly, you are the Son of God!" *(Have the children jump up and clap.)*

Jesus Walks on the Water— A Puppet Craft

Kids will enjoy creating this simple project to help them remember the story of Jesus walking on the water. Each child will need a large white paper plate with two small one-half-inch slits cut in it, three craft sticks, and a small construction paper boat. You'll also need glue, scissors, and markers.

Before you begin the story, have children each do the following:

● Color half of the plate blue to represent the water, covering the slits.

● Glue a craft stick to the back of the construction paper boat.

● Draw faces on the tops of two craft sticks.

When the children are finished making their crafts, tell this story:

The disciples went into the boat while Jesus prayed. *(Place the boat through the slit on one side of the paper.)*

It became windy, and the wind blew the boat away from the land. *(Move the boat back and forth in the water.)*

In the morning, Jesus came out to the disciples by walking on the water. *(Glue Jesus onto the water.)*

The disciples were scared, but Jesus said, "Don't be afraid!"

Peter said, "Lord, I want to come out to you and walk on the water, too!" So Jesus said "Come!" *(Place Peter through the slit in the center of the paper.)*

When Peter got out of the boat, it became windy again! *(Move the boat back and forth in the water.)*

Peter began to sink, and he called out to Jesus, "Lord, save me!" *(Push Peter down through the slit in the paper.)*

Jesus reached out his hand to save Peter and asked him, "Why did you doubt?" *(Pull Peter up out of the slit.)*

The disciples said to Jesus, "Truly, you are the Son of God!" *(Move Peter up and down happily in the boat.)*

Jesus Visits Mary and Martha

Luke 10:38-42

Mary and Martha both had good intentions. Mary was eager to listen to Jesus' words and soak up his wisdom. Martha was eager to serve her Lord with comfortable furnishings and a good home-cooked meal. It's hard to fault Martha, yet Jesus said that Mary chose what was better.

The preschoolers in your class aren't likely to have the same worries about setting priorities that adults have. However, even young children can learn that it's good to always put Jesus first. Use these activities to teach children that learning about Jesus is always a good choice.

Mary and Martha Chant

Kids will enjoy doing this familiar chant while learning about the story of Mary and Martha. Begin by asking kids to clap their hands together and then slap their knees, clap their hands together and slap their knees, and so on, until they have picked up on the beat. Then sing the following chant with the same rhythm as "Who Stole the Cookies?"

> **Who sat with Jesus when he came to visit?**
> **Mary sat with Jesus when he came to visit!**
> **Who, Mary? Yes, Mary!**
> **I agree! It's true!**
>
> **Who was too busy to hear Jesus talk?**
> **Martha was too busy to hear Jesus talk!**
> **Who, Martha? Yes, Martha!**
> **I agree! It's true!**

Who knows that we must listen when Jesus talks?
I know that I must listen when Jesus talks!
Who, me? Yes, you!
I agree! It's true!

Here Is Martha, Here Is Mary

This finger play is similar to "Where Is Thumbkin?" Have the children mimic your actions. Then teach them the words.

Here is Martha. *("Walk" one thumb.)*
Here is Martha. *(Walk one thumb.)*
Watch her work. *(Make "binocular" eyes.)*
Watch her work. *(Make binocular eyes.)*
She is always scrubbing. *(Pretend to scrub.)*
She is always cooking. *(Pretend to stir.)*
For her friend Jesus. *(Point up.)*
For her friend Jesus. *(Point up.)*

Here is Mary. *("Walk" the other thumb.)*
Here is Mary. *(Walk the other thumb.)*
She's so calm. *(Put your finger to your lips.)*
She's so still. *(Stand very still.)*
Listening to Jesus. *(Cup your ear with your hand.)*
Listening to Jesus. *(Cup your ear with your hand.)*
His words are dear. *(Cross your hands on your heart.)*
His words are dear. *(Cross your hands on your heart.)*

Here is Jesus. *("Walk" your pointer finger.)*
Here is Jesus. *(Walk your pointer finger.)*
He loves Martha. *(Hug yourself.)*
He loves Mary. *(Hug yourself.)*
But Mary chose what's best. *(Wiggle the "Mary" thumb.)*
But Mary chose what's best. *(Wiggle the "Mary" thumb.)*
She listened to him. *(Cup your ear with your hand.)*
She listened to him. *(Cup your ear with your hand.)*

Jesus Is Coming

Have the children act out this action rhyme while you say the words.

Hello! I'm Martha *(wave one hand)*,
And I'm Mary. *(Wave the other hand.)*

We're excited because *(clap your hands)*
Jesus is coming! *(Raise both hands and "twinkle" your fingers.)*

Martha said *(wave "Martha" hand):*
"I can't wait until Jesus comes. *(Put your hands to your cheeks.)*
But I have so much to do. *(Hold your arms out from your sides.)*
I need to clean the house *(pretend to polish)*
And sweep the floor *(pretend to sweep)*
And cook the meal. *(Pretend to stir.)*
I wish Mary would help me because *(put your hands on your hips)*
Jesus is coming!" *(Raise both hands and "twinkle" your fingers.)*

And Mary said *(Wave "Mary" hand):*
"I'm so glad because Jesus is here. *("Paint" a smile on your face.)*
I've looked forward to his visit for so long. *(Extend your hands.)*
I want to talk to Jesus *(move your fingers and thumb in a "talk-
    ing" motion)*
And listen to his words. *(Cup your ear with your hand.)*
Jesus is wise and wonderful. *(Point up.)*
I wish Martha would sit and listen because *(put your hands on
    your hips)*
Jesus is here!" *(Raise your arms and "twinkle" hands.)*

And Jesus said *(stand up tall):*
"I'm happy to visit my friends Mary and Martha. *("Paint" a
    smile on your face.)*
They're dear, dear friends. *(Put your hands over your heart.)*
Martha has worked so hard. *(Pretend to scrub.)*
But Mary is ready to listen. *(Cup your ear with your hand.)*
I love them both *(hug yourself),*
But Mary has chosen what is best. *(Raise your pointer finger.)*
And it will never be taken away." *(Shake your head.)*

This Is the Way

Sing this song to the tune of "Here We Go 'Round the Mulberry Bush." Have the children pantomime the actions of each verse. After you sing each verse, ask if the verse describes Mary or Martha.

This is the way we dust and sweep,
Dust and sweep, dust and sweep.
This is the way we dust and sweep.
Jesus is coming!

This is the way we cook and bake,
Cook and bake, cook and bake.
This is the way we cook and bake.
Jesus is coming!

This is the way we sit and listen,
Sit and listen, sit and listen.
This is the way we sit and listen
To Jesus' words.

Jesus Teaches Us to Pray

Matthew 6:9-13

Your little ones may have learned prayers for bedtime and prayers for mealtime, and some may have learned to talk to God any time! The Lord's Prayer gives all believers an example of how we can stand face to face with the God of the Universe and talk to him about our daily needs. Use these activities to help preschoolers remember that God is listening to them!

Action Prayer

This action prayer will help your kids remember the basics Jesus taught about prayer. This version of the Lord's Prayer is adapted from the New Century Version of Luke 11:1-4. It will help children understand what the prayer means.

To do this action prayer, say the words that appear in bold type and have the children repeat them with you. Then practice doing the motions with the words.

Action 1:

God, your name is holy!

Holy, holy, holy; your name is holy! (*Start in a crouching position. Move up a little on each "holy," then crouch back down and jump up high on the last word.*)

Action 2:

Let your kingdom come. (*Have each preschooler place his or her hands on the shoulders of another to form a train. When everyone is connected, have kids march around the room saying, "Let your kingdom come, come!" to the rhythm of "Chugga, chugga, choo, choo!"*)

Action 3:

Give us the food we need each day. *(Have the kids each make a bowl with one hand and a spoon out of the other hand and pantomime eating.)*

Action 4:

Forgive us as we forgive others. *(Have the kids join hands to form a circle. Sing this song to the tune of "The Bear Went Over the Mountain.")*

Forgive as we forgive others *(raise hands up together and walk to center of circle),*
Forgive as we forgive others *(bring hands down and walk back),*
Forgive as we forgive others *(raise hands up together and walk to the center);*
And show the world your love. *(Drop hands and hug the person on your right, then the person on your left.)*

A Prayer Song

Sing this song to the tune of "Jesus Loves Me" to help familiarize children with the King James vocabulary of the traditional Lord's Prayer. Explain unfamiliar terms before you sing together. Be sure to sing the chorus between verses.

Our Father which art in heaven *(make a "house" by touching your fingertips together),*
Hallowed be thy name, dear Lord. *(Lift your hands.)*
Thy kingdom come; thy will be done. *(Turn your hands palm-down and wiggle your fingers as you spread your hands apart to the sides.)*
These are words taught by your Son. *(Touch your middle fingers to the palms of the opposite hands to sign "Jesus.")*

Chorus:

Teach us to pray, Lord. *(Touch your palms together in front of your chest.)*
Teach us to pray, Lord. *(Touch your palms together in front of your chest.)*
Teach us to pray, Lord *(touch your palms together in front of your chest),*
So we can honor you. *(Bow down on one knee, and stand back up.)*

Give this day our daily bread *(pretend to eat);*
Only by your hand we're fed. *(Point up.)*

Forgive us as we forgive. *(Hold out one hand to the side with the palm up, then the other hand.)*

Show us, Lord, how we should live. *(Lift your hands in front of you.)*

Lead us not to temptation. *(Tiptoe in place.)*

Deliver from the evil one. *(Jump back.)*

Thine forever the kingdom *(point up, then make a "crown" for your head with your hands),*

Power, and Glory; let them come! *(Flex muscles, then lift your hands, making fingers "twinkle" down to sides.)*

Teaching the Master's Prayer

When Jesus' disciples learned how to pray, they probably learned the reasons behind each part of the prayer. The words of the traditional Lord's Prayer are too hard for preschoolers—they won't be able to grasp the meaning without your help. Help your preschoolers understand the Lord's Prayer with this guided-action response.

Explain all the words and the actions just as they're written here. Then after practicing several times, just say each line of the Lord's Prayer and have the children do the actions. Soon they will have learned the entire prayer.

Reach up to a loving daddy when you say "Our Father." *(Reach up.)*

"Which art in heaven" means God lives somewhere we can't see with our eyes. *(Look up, down, and all around to try to see heaven.)*

"Hallowed be thy name" means that God is special. God is more special than anyone because he is God. Let's clap for God. *(Applaud.)*

"Thy kingdom come. Thy will be done" means we want to do things God's way. *(Have kids point up.)*

Show the mountains of earth when you say "on earth" and the clouds of the sky when you say "as it is in heaven." *(Kids each use one hand to make rolling hills and the other to "feel" the clouds of heaven.)*

Pretend you're eating a sandwich as you say, "Give us this day our daily bread." *(Use both hands and take an imaginary bite.)*

"And forgive us our trespasses" means we need to be sorry for the wrong things we do. *(Make a sad face.)*

"As we forgive those who trespass against us" reminds us that we need to forgive other people when they do things that hurt us. *(Rub your chest in a small circular motion to show forgiveness.)*

"And lead us not into temptation, but deliver us from evil": tells God that we want to obey him. Make angel wings to remind you of goodness. *(Flap your "wings.")*

"For thine is the kingdom, and the power, and the glory, forever" tells us about three things God has. First, everything in the world belongs to God. Second, God is very strong. And third, God is glorious. *(Have each child pantomime picking up something, then holding it up to God for the word "kingdom." For the word "power," have everyone make muscles. For the word "glory," have the children raise their hands and "twinkle" their fingers.)*

Hands in Prayer

In the Luke 11:1-4 version of the Lord's Prayer, the disciples asked for help in learning to pray and they were given a pattern. Help your preschoolers learn how the Lord's Prayer was given to Jesus' followers with this hands-only action rhyme.

Jesus taught his friends to pray *(place your palms together, like praying hands)*
About these five things every day *(hold one hand up with fingers spread apart):*

God is holy, number one. *(Touch your thumb.)*
His kingdom come, his will be done. *(Touch your index finger.)*

Give us all our daily needs. *(Touch your middle finger.)*
That is subject number three.

Four, forgive us all our sins. *(Touch your ring finger.)*
Five, all glory belongs to him. *(Touch your pinkie.)*

I am learning how to pray *(point to yourself)*
About these five things every day. *(Run your index finger along the five fingers.)*

I count up, and when I'm done *(touch each finger individually from thumb to pinkie),*

I remember that I love God's Son. *(Make a heart shape by putting the heels of your hands together with the thumbs up and the fingers bent at the second knuckles with nail-tips touching.)*

Jesus Heals Ten Lepers

Luke
17:11-19

Jesus healed ten lepers, but only one came back to say "Thank you." A thankful heart is precious to Jesus. Jesus was pleased with the man who said "Thank you" just as he is pleased with our thankfulness.

Enjoy these activities with the preschoolers in your class. Once they learn what it means to be thankful, they'll be enthusiastically thankful for everything.

Teacher Tip

Preschool children will not know what leprosy is, so explain that it is a bad skin disease. In Bible times, there was no medicine to cure it and people were afraid they might catch it. So the "lepers" had to live outside the towns all by themselves.

Ten Sad Lepers

Before teaching this poem, have the children practice all the motions. Then as they learn the words, they can do the appropriate motions. If there are ten children in the class, line them up and have the first one run back to his seat, the second one leap back, the third one skip back, and so on.

Ten sad lepers outside the town did roam.
(Hold up ten fingers.)
They wanted to be healed so they could all go home. *(Hold out your hands.)*

They said to Jesus, "Please heal us, sir." *(Clasp your hands together as if begging.)*
He said to see the priest, and they were off in a blur. *(Nod your head and point your arm away from your body.)*

The first one ran, the second one leapt *(run in place, then leap),*
The third one skipped, the fourth one crept. *(Skip in place, then creep in place.)*

The fifth one stumbled over sticks and rocks *(pretend to stumble),*
The sixth one limped away in holey socks. *(Limp in place.)*

The seventh one jumped, the eighth one slid *(jump and then pretend to slide),*
The ninth one tiptoed; oh yes, he did. *(Tiptoe in place.)*

But the tenth one, the tenth one, he said "no" to fun. *(Hold up ten fingers, then shake your head.)*
He came back to Jesus, God's only Son. *(Walk in place.)*

"Thank you, Lord, for healing my skin." *(Clasp your hands together in thanks.)*
His thankful heart made Jesus grin. *(Fold your arms across your chest and nod and smile.)*

The Ten Lepers Finger Play

Ten lepers, ten fingers…a perfect match! In this finger play, the children will hold up all ten fingers for the first two lines. Then they will each use one pointer to point to the thumb on the other hand and push it down. They will do the same for the pointer, the middle finger, the ring finger, and the pinkie. When all those fingers are down, they will use the pointer on that hand to point and push down the other hand's thumb, pointer, middle finger, and ring finger, but not the pinkie.

Ten sad lepers were on the road. *(Hold up all ten fingers.)*
Jesus healed them all. *(Hug yourself.)*

This one ran away and said nothing. *(Point to your thumb and push it down.)*

This one ran away and said nothing. *(Point to your pointer finger and push it down.)*

This one ran away and said nothing. *(Point to your middle finger and push it down.)*

This one ran away and said nothing. *(Point to your ring finger and push it down.)*

This one ran away and said nothing. *(Point to your pinkie and push it down.)*

This one ran away and said nothing. *(Point to your other thumb and push it down.)*

This one ran away and said nothing. *(Point to your other pointer and push it down.)*

This one ran away and said nothing. *(Point to your other middle finger and push it down.)*

This one ran away and said nothing. *(Point to your other ring finger and push it down.)*

But this one ran away and came back to say "Thank you" *(point to your other pinkie);*

He said "Thank you" to Jesus. "Thank you, Lord!" *(Clasp your hands in thanks.)*

Not Thankful; Not Thankful; Thankful

This game is similar to Duck, Duck, Goose—a favorite game of preschoolers everywhere.

Seat the children in a circle. Choose one child to be It. Say: **One day, Jesus met ten lepers on the road. They asked to be healed. Jesus told them to go see the priest. On their way there, the lepers were healed. Nine of them ran away home, but the tenth man came back to thank Jesus. Who was the thankful one?**

This question is Its cue to walk around the room, tapping children on the head. It says, "Not thankful; not thankful; not thankful" as he or she taps the children on the head. When It taps a child and says "Thankful," that child jumps up and chases It around the circle back to the empty space. Then the children in the circle all say, "Thank you, Jesus." Choose another It for the next round.

The Ten Lepers Drama

Children will enjoy acting out this story. Read the story and do the motions. The children will easily follow your lead.

Jesus was walking down the road. *(Walk in place.)*
He heard something. *(Hold your hand to your ear and cock your head.)*
It was ten lepers. *(Hold up ten fingers.)*
They were jumping up and down! *(Jump up and down.)*

"Jesus, Jesus, help us!" they called. *(Put your hands to your mouth and call, "Jesus, help us!")*

Jesus said, "Go to the priest." *(Point your arm with your hand and finger straight out.)*

So they walked to the priest. *(Walk in place.)*

As they walked, they looked at their hands. *(Look at your hands.)*

They looked at their feet. *(Look at your feet.)*

They were healed! *(Clap your hands and jump.)*

Nine lepers ran home. *(Run in place.)*

But one leper turned around. *(Turn around.)*

And ran back to Jesus. *(Run in place.)*

He got down on his knees *(kneel down)*

And thanked God for healing him. *(Clasp your hands together in prayer.)*

"Thank you, Jesus!" *(Keep your hands clasped together.)*

Jesus said, "Didn't I heal ten men?" *(Hold up ten fingers.)*

"Why did only one say 'Thank you?' " *(Hold up one finger.)*

Jesus Blesses the Children

Mark 10:13-16

J esus gave children a special place in his earthly ministry. He taught that they are models for adults! We each need a child-like spirit of trust, freedom, and willingness to learn in our too-hectic schedules. Preschoolers will love learning that the Creator of all the universe especially loved little children. Enjoy your preschoolers as you revel together in Jesus' love!

And It Makes Me Want to Dance

Encourage free expression of movement as you finish each stanza of this story. Use a cassette tape with a variety of musical styles. Play it low in the background, raising the volume to cue the children to dance! Lower it again as their cue to freeze. Have a lot of fun with this activity by varying the pace of the last line, building anticipation for movement!

Parents brought their children (*walk around the room pantomiming holding little hands*)
To sit in Jesus' lap. (*Pantomime picking up a child and lifting him or her up to Jesus.*)
Jesus loves the children,
And it makes me want to dance! (*Allow for free movement.*)

The disciples got too grumpy (*make a grouchy face*),
But Jesus set them straight. (*Stand up very straight and still.*)
Jesus loves the children,
And it makes me want to dance! (*Allow for free movement.*)

Jesus blessed the children (*reach out and pantomime touching children's heads*)

With a touch and a word. *(Hold hands with a friend.)*
Jesus loves the children,
And it makes me want to dance! *(Allow for free movement with partners.)*

Although I sometimes wiggle *(wiggle around)*
Every time I get the chance *(wiggle around more)*,
I remember Jesus loves me *(stop and be still except for a tap on your temple)*—
And it makes me want to dance! *(Allow for free movement.)*

The Children's Trip to Jesus

Have the children repeat your actions in this joyful journey to Jesus.

One day, some parents got ready to take their children to see Jesus. "Come on! Let's go!" *(Motion to come with your whole arm.)*

First, they shuffled through the dusty streets of their city. *(Brush your palms away from each other to make a "dusty"-sounding rhythm.)*

When they came to the edge of town, they had to pass through grassy fields. *(Rub tips of your fingers with the thumbs of both hands.)*

Soon they came to a hill that they had to climb. *(Pretend to climb to the top of a hill.)*

They could see a crowd of people in the distance. *(Shield your eyes and point.)*

The adults ran down the hill. *(Lean forward and run in place.)*
The children rolled down the hill. *(Roll your arms in a circle.)*
When they reached the crowd, they were out of breath. *(Pant.)*
Whew! They were finally there! *(Wipe your brow.)*
They tried to get through the crowd. *("Push" with palms and elbows.)*

"Where do you think you're going?" the disciples said. *(Repeat the line in a booming voice.)*

"To Jesus!" the travelers said. *(Repeat the line in a squeaky voice.)*
"No, you're not!" *(Shake your head.)*
"Yes, we are!" *(Nod your head.)*
"What is happening?" asked Jesus. *(Shrug your shoulders to ask a question.)*

The travelers said: "We have been on dusty roads *(brush your palms together)*
And through grassy fields. *(Rub your fingertips with both thumbs.)*
We've climbed up hills *(climb)*;

We've rolled down hills. *("Roll" your forearms.)*
And we've pushed through crowds. *(Push with palms and elbows.)*
And now that our journey's ended, we'd like to see Jesus, please." *(Clasp your hands together.)*
"I am he. *(Point to yourself.)*
Let the children come to me *(beckon with your arms)*,
Because I love them so." *(Hug yourself.)*
And the children went to him.

Hum, Hum, Let the Children Come

Kids will remember the message of this funky song long after their lesson! Sing it to the tune of "Louie, Louie." If you don't know this tune, your youth leader may know it as "Pharaoh, Pharaoh." The melody is very repetitive—a good thing for young singers. Begin by having the children do the actions while you sing the melody slowly and gently. Then have children learn the chorus. Before you know it, they'll know the whole song.

Chorus:
Don't look so glum. *(Show a scowling face.)*
No, friends *(pump your fists at your sides, like a "choo-choo" train's movement)*—
Let the children come! *(Roll your forearms toward yourself.)*
Oh, how I love them! *(Hug yourself first with one arm, then cross the other arm over.)*
Don't look so glum. *(Show a scowling face.)*
No, friends *(hold your fists at your sides, like a choo-choo train's movement)*—
Let the children come! *(Roll your forearms toward yourself.)*
Ooo-oo-oo-oo

Verse:
Some people once brought their children to Jesus *(pat the air at the height of a child)*
So they could be touched by his loving hand. *(Touch one forearm with your palm.)*
The disciples said "No, he's too busy for you." *(Shake your head.)*
But Jesus just smiled and he kept on saying *("draw" a smile on your face)*—

(Repeat chorus)

I Love Him and He Loves Me

Sing this song to the tune of "Twinkle, Twinkle, Little Star." It can also be a chanted finger-rhyme.

I love him and he loves me *(point to yourself, cross your arms over your chest and point up, and cross your arms and point to yourself)*;
That's how it will always be. *(Make big arm circles.)*
The disciples said, "No, go away! *(Pretend to shoo children away.)*
He doesn't have time for you today!" *(Point to an imaginary watch.)*
I love him and he loves me *(point to yourself, cross your arms over your chest and point up, and cross your arms and point to yourself)*;
That's how it will always be. *(Make big arm circles.)*

I love him and he loves me *(point to yourself, cross your arms over your chest and point up, and cross your arms and point to yourself)*;
That's how it will always be. *(Make big arm circles.)*
Jesus said, "Let the children come to me *(beckon with your arm)*;
The kingdom's filled with the likes of these." *(Point around the room with your index finger.)*
I love him and he loves me *(point to yourself, cross your arms over your chest and point up, and cross your arms and point to yourself)*;
That's how it will always be. *(Make big arm circles.)*

Jesus Meets Zacchaeus

Luke 19:1-10

What child can't relate to being too small to see something he or she wants to see? Small-in-stature Zacchaeus had the same problem, but he used imagination and determination to find a way to get past the crowd and see Jesus. And Jesus changed Zacchaeus' life!

Each preschooler's life will be changed also, as he or she meets Jesus and learns of his love and care. Use the following activities to help your children "see" Jesus.

Sitting in a Tree

This singsong rhyme is great fun! Each child does all the actions while you recite the verse.

Poor little Zacchaeus, small as he could be (*hold your hand up and point to your pinkie*),

Wanted to see Jesus but was too short to see. (*Shrug your shoulders with your palms up.*)

A thought came to him; he remembered a tree. (*Tap your finger on the side of your head.*)

He could run and climb it, and then he could see. (*Pretend to climb a tree.*)

So he did just that, and he sat to wait (*cross your hands in front of your chest*),

Hoping to see Jesus before it got too late. (*Shade your eyes and move your head slowly from one side to the other.*)

When Jesus came by, to Zacchaeus he said *("walk" your fingers in front of you),*
"Let's go to your house and eat some bread!" *(Cup your hands to your mouth.)*

So he went with Jesus and they ate dinner *(march your feet),*
And he learned that night that he was a sinner. *(Put your hands on your chest.)*

Zacchaeus decided that very day *(clap your hands)*
To trust in Jesus and to always obey. *(Point up.)*

Go, Zacchaeus, Find a Tree

This is a fast-paced game, meant to be played outside. It is similar to the game Squirrels in a Tree—children won't want to be caught without trees.

Form groups of three. Have two children in each group hold hands as they would if they were the "bridge" in "London Bridge." These pairs are the "trees" in this game. The third child in each trio is "Zacchaeus." This game works well if your class is evenly divided by three. It works even better if you have one additional child—he or she will also be a Zacchaeus. If you have two extra children, play the game yourself and be part of a tree.

Have the trees hold hands and hold their arms up high. Have the Zacchaeuses wander around the room while you say: **One day, Jesus was coming to town. Zacchaeus wanted to see Jesus with all his heart. But Zacchaeus was too short to see Jesus over the crowds of people. Then he had an idea. He would climb up a sycamore tree. Here comes Jesus. Hurry, Zacchaeus—find a tree!**

That's the cue for each Zacchaeus to run to the nearest tree and stand "inside" the tree. The trees drop their arms to "fence in" the Zacchaeuses. When each Zacchaeus has found a tree, say: **Jesus walked into town, and Zacchaeus could see him. Jesus saw Zacchaeus, too. Jesus walked over to the sycamore tree and said: "Zacchaeus, you come down. I want to go to your house for dinner today."**

Then call out, "Zacchaeus, you come down," and have the trees release the Zacchaeuses to roam around again for another round of play. If there is an extra child, he or she calls out, "Zacchaeus, you come down."

After several rounds, have the Zacchaeuses trade places with the trees.

For extra fun, at the end of the game, serve a snack and tell the rest of the story.

I Am Zacchaeus

Children will have fun identifying with Zacchaeus as he struggles to see Jesus. In this action rhyme, each child acts out the story while you recite the words.

I am Zacchaeus. *(Point to yourself.)*
I want to see Jesus. *(Shade your eyes with your hand.)*
But I'm too short to see him. *(Hold your hand out to your side at waist level.)*
Maybe if I jump I'll see him. *(Jump.)*
No, I still can't see him. *(Shake your head.)*
Maybe if I scrunch real low and peek through people's legs, I'll see him. *(Scrunch down low and pretend to peek through legs.)*
No, I still can't see! *(Shake your head.)*
How am I ever going to see Jesus? *(Shrug your shoulders.)*
I know! I'll climb that big tree. *(Pretend to climb tree.)*
Hey! The view's great. Now I'm sure to see Jesus! *(Make "binocular" eyes.)*
I see him! He sees me, too! *(Wave to Jesus.)*
Jesus says he's coming to my house! I'd better hurry down. *(Pretend to climb down the tree.)*
I'm so glad I climbed that tree. I got to meet Jesus! *(Hug yourself.)*

Zacchaeus Song

Children will enjoy this musical version of Zacchaeus' story. Sing it to the tune of "I'm a Little Teapot."

I am Zacchaeus, short and small. *(Pat the air near to the ground.)*
I want to see Jesus, but the people are too tall. *(Pat the air above your head.)*
Maybe if I climb that sycamore tree *(pretend to climb)*,
I'll see Jesus and he'll see me. *(Point away from yourself, then point to yourself.)*

Up I climbed and I took my seat *(pretend to sit down)*,
And there was the Lord I wanted to meet. *(Wave to Jesus.)*
Jesus said, "Come down! At your house I'll stay" *(beckon with
  your hand)*,
So down I came and we went on our way. *(Pump your arms at
  your sides as if walking briskly.)*

Jesus Heals a Blind Man

Mark
10:46-52

Children, even very young children, need to hear about Jesus' healing power. The story of Jesus helping the blind man in Jericho can be a real tool in teaching your children that Jesus really cares about them, just as he cared for the blind man.

This story can also serve as a powerful introduction to the concept of faith and thankfulness. Use these activities to teach the specific Bible story or any time you want to talk about Jesus' miracles.

Blind-Man Rhyme

Children will enjoy reciting this fun rhyme about the blind man Jesus healed in Jericho. Lead the children through the rhyme several times to help them learn the words and actions.

Encourage children to teach the rhyme to their families. They'll be having so much fun, they won't even realize that they're rooting the Bible story in their hearts and sharing it with others!

There was a man very long ago *(put your hands on your hips);*
His friends all called him Bart. *(Give your neighbor a high five.)*
He begged all day in Jericho. *(Cup your hands in front of you.)*
It was enough to break your heart. *(Shake your head sadly.)*

You see, poor Bart was blind as could be. *(Point to your eyes.)*
He couldn't see at all. *(Put your hands over your eyes.)*
A man was coming who could make the blind see! *(Point down the road.)*
Bart started to shout and call! *(Cup your hands around your mouth.)*

Bart yelled out, "Have mercy on me!" *(Stretch out your arms in front of you.)*

And Jesus stopped to say *(walk in place, then stop)*,
"Your faith is strong. I'll make you see." *(Pretend to look through binoculars.)*
Bart's eyes were healed right away! *(Clap your hands.)*

But old Bart's story didn't end right there. *(Shake your head "no.")*
That's not what the Bible says. *(Hold your hands like an open book.)*
For Bart found that Jesus really cares *(put your hands over your heart),*
So he followed him all of his days. *(Walk in place.)*

Blind-Man Song

Teach the children the actions to this song. Have the children do the actions while you sing the song. After you've sung it a few times, the children will start to pick up the words.

Sing these original words to the familiar tune of "Blindman." If you don't know this tune, the youth leader in your church can probably help you with it. If you have a copy of *The Group Songbook*, this melody is number 45.

The blind man stood by the road and he cried. *(Rub your eyes as if you're crying.)*
The blind man said, "Please have mercy on me." *(Clasp your hands together as if you're begging.)*
The people said, "Be quiet"—they were mean to him. *(Wag your finger.)*
But Jesus sa-ai-id *(put your hands around your mouth to "call"),*
"Blind man, come he-re-re *(beckon with your hand),*
Blind man, come he-re-re *(beckon with your hand),*
Blind man, come he-re-re *(beckon with your hand);*
I think I can help." *(Nod your head.)*

The people said, "Hey blind man, Jesus called for you." *(Beckon with your hand.)*
The blind man jumped right up and went to Jesus' side. *(Jump up and pump your arms as if you're running.)*
He said, "Please, Jesus, won't you heal my eyes?" *(Clasp your hands together as if you're begging.)*
And Jesus sa-ai-id *(put your hands to your mouth as if to call),*
"Your faith has healed you *(use your hands as "binoculars"),*
Your faith has healed you *(use your hands as binoculars),*

Your faith has healed you (*use your hands as binoculars*);
Now follow me." (*Beckon with your hand.*)
"Thank you!" (*Clap on each word.*)

Where Is Jesus?

Teach children the following simple song to remind them of Jesus' healing power. Tell them to pretend that they are Bartimaeus. During the first verse, have the children cover their eyes with one hand and reach out with the other hand as if searching for Jesus. During the second verse, have them uncover their eyes and clap along with the beat. Sing the song to the tune of "Frère Jacques."

Where is Jesus?
Where is Jesus?
I can't see.
I can't see.
Jesus can do anything.
Jesus can do anything.
He'll make me see.
He'll make me see.

Now here's Jesus.
Now here's Jesus.
I can see!
I can see!
Jesus can do anything.
Jesus can do anything.
He healed me.
He healed me.

Following Jesus

Often when we tell the story of Jesus healing the blind man in Jericho, we focus on the miracle itself. In this fun interactive story, we'll look at what Bartimaeus did after Jesus healed him.

The Bible says the blind man "received his sight and followed Jesus along the road." Help your preschoolers learn to be thankful for Jesus' love and to follow him in all they do.

Have the children sit in a group on the floor. Sit opposite them and tell the following story. The first time you say the name "Jesus" during the story, jump up and repeat this rhyme:

Following, following Jesus;
That's what I want to do!
Following, following Jesus;
Won't you follow him, too?

At the end of the rhyme, point to a child and have that child come sit next to you for the rest of the story.

The next time you say "Jesus," repeat the rhyme with the child sitting next to you and have that child choose another child to join you both. Continue the process throughout the story, always letting the last child chosen pick the next child.

Teacher Tip

If you have a large class, choose two or more children to join you at a time. If you have a very small class, modify the story so you say "Jesus" the same number of times as there are children present.

Tell the following story:

One day a long, long time ago, a blind man was sitting by the side of the road. A large crowd of people was coming along the road. And at the center of the crowd was Jesus. *(Repeat rhyme.)*

The blind man became very excited! He had heard that this was a man who could do wonderful, amazing things. He had heard about Jesus! *(Repeat rhyme.)*

So the blind man called out for help. "Have mercy on me," he cried. "Please have mercy on me, Jesus." *(Repeat rhyme.)*

The people standing near the blind man told him to be quiet. "Stop yelling," they told him. "You're too noisy. You're bothering Jesus." *(Repeat rhyme.)*

But the blind man just yelled louder and louder. And what do you think happened? The crowd stopped because they heard a voice. They heard a man say, "Call him." And who do you think was calling for the blind man? It was Jesus! *(Repeat rhyme.)*

The people said to the blind man, "Cheer up! Get on your feet. He's calling you." So the blind man stood up and walked over to Jesus. *(Repeat rhyme.)*

The crowd became very quiet. They wanted to see what would happen.

"What do you want me to do for you?" asked Jesus. *(Repeat rhyme.)*

"Rabbi," said the blind man, "I want to see."

Now the crowd didn't make a sound at all. Everyone watched and waited.

"Go, your faith has made you well," said Jesus. *(Repeat rhyme.)*

And just like that, the blind man could see! He was so happy, he decided to follow Jesus! *(Repeat rhyme.)*

For extra fun when the story is over, lead your class in a march around the room as you all repeat the rhyme together.

Jesus Enters Jerusalem

Matthew
21:1-11

Children love to celebrate!
They love birthdays, holidays, family parties, and other special days throughout the year. In fact, young children don't need much prompting at all to swing into a celebration.

Make use of all that natural exuberance as you teach the story of Jesus' triumphal entry into Jerusalem. Use the following activities to help your children join with the townspeople of Jerusalem as they celebrate that Jesus is king!

Hosanna Hum-Along

You'll need a tricycle or some other kind of children's riding-toy for this activity. Choose a volunteer to ride the tricycle at the start of the parade. Have the children pretend that the tricycle is the donkey and that the tricycle rider is Jesus. Have "Jesus" lead the rest of the children in a Palm Sunday parade.

While the children are marching around the room, have them sing the following song to the tune of "Old MacDonald Had a Farm."

After children have learned the words to the song, introduce this fun variation. Sing the song through the first time. The next time through, hum the first line of the song instead of singing it. Next time, hum the second line, and so on, until you've got an "instrumental" melody!

Have the children take turns riding the tricycle and leading the parade.

Here comes Jesus. Hail the king!
Ho-san-na to him!

Here comes Jesus. Let's all sing
Ho-san-na to him!

Here he comes,
God's own Son.
Sing his praises,
Everyone.

Here comes Jesus. Let's all sing
Ho-san-na to him!

Palm Sunday Finger Play

Lead children in the following fun finger play. Repeat the rhyme several times so children can learn the words and motions.

One little child by the side of the road (*hold up one finger*)
Waited for Jesus to pass. (*Shield your eyes as if looking down the road.*)
He waved his palm branch in the air (*wave your arms up and down*),
'Cause Jesus had come at last. (*Clap your hands.*)

Repeat the rhyme, holding up two, three, four, and five fingers each time. (For extra fun, say the rhyme as many times as there are children in your class. You might want to have a child step forward each time a new number is introduced.)

End the finger play with this verse:

Crowds of people by the side of the road (*flash ten fingers several times*)
Waited for Jesus to pass. (*Shield your eyes as if looking down the road.*)
They knew Jesus was the promised king. (*Point to heaven.*)
They were glad he had come at last! (*Clap your hands.*)

The Droopy Donkey

Kids will love acting out this simple drama, told from the point of view of the donkey chosen to carry Jesus into Jerusalem.

Before the story, photocopy the "Droopy Donkey Ears" handout on page 81. You'll need one set of ears for each child. You'll also need a construction paper headband for each child.

Have children each cut out a set of ears. Then show children how to use tape to attach the ears to their headbands. After everyone has finished, help children don their donkey ears. Sit on the floor with your group and teach them the actions of the story. Have them repeat the story with you several times until they're familiar with the words and actions.

Hello. I'm Donny the Donkey. *(Wave.)*

People call me Droopy because of my ears. *(Gently shake your head to wiggle the ears.)*

They also call me Droopy 'cause I've been sad lately. *(Make a sad face.)*

You see, no one ever rides me, and I don't know why. *(Shrug your shoulders.)*

I have a very strong back *(flex your arms),*

And I'm very gentle. *(Fold your hands.)*

But no one ever rides me. *(Shake your head sadly.)*

I go to the market and offer to carry bags of grain *(crawl on all fours to one side of the room),*

And I go to the well and offer to carry jugs of water *(crawl to the other side of the room),*

But no one pays any attention to me. *(Crawl sadly back to original location.)*

My mom says God must be saving me for something special. *(Point to heaven.)*

I sure hope so! *(Make praying hands.)*

Hey, look! Who are those men? *(Point into distance.)*

And what are they saying to my owners? *(Cup your hand to your ear.)*

Can it be? The Master needs me? *(Look very surprised.)*

Jesus wants to ride me into Jerusalem? *(Crawl in place.)*

Me?? *(Point to yourself.)*

Wow! My mom was right! God *does* have a plan for me! *(Point to heaven.)*

Sorry—gotta go! I've got a very special job to do! 'Bye! *(Wave goodbye.)*

Paper Praises

Give children crepe paper streamers to use as Paper Praisers in this action rhyme. Or let children cut out simple palm fronds from green construction paper. (Very young children can simply wave sheets of green construction paper.)

Have children line up on either side of an imaginary road in your classroom. (To help kids envision Jesus' triumphal entry into Jerusalem, you may want to outline a road on your classroom floor with masking tape.)

To begin, have children place their Paper Praisers on the floor in front of them. Repeat the rhyme several times so children can learn the actions and words.

> **We're waiting, waiting for Jesus.** *(Put your hand over your eyes, looking into the distance.)*
> **We heard he's coming this way.** *(Pretend to talk to each other.)*
> **We know that he's been sent by God.** *(Point to heaven.)*
> **What a special day!** *(Clap your hands in excitement.)*
>
> **Oh, look! I see him coming!** *(Point down the road.)*
> **Let's all praise his name!** *(Pick up Paper Praisers.)*
> **Hooray! Hooray for Jesus!** *(Wave Paper Praisers up and down.)*
> **We're so glad he came!** *(Shake Paper Praisers together.)*

Droopy Donkey Ears

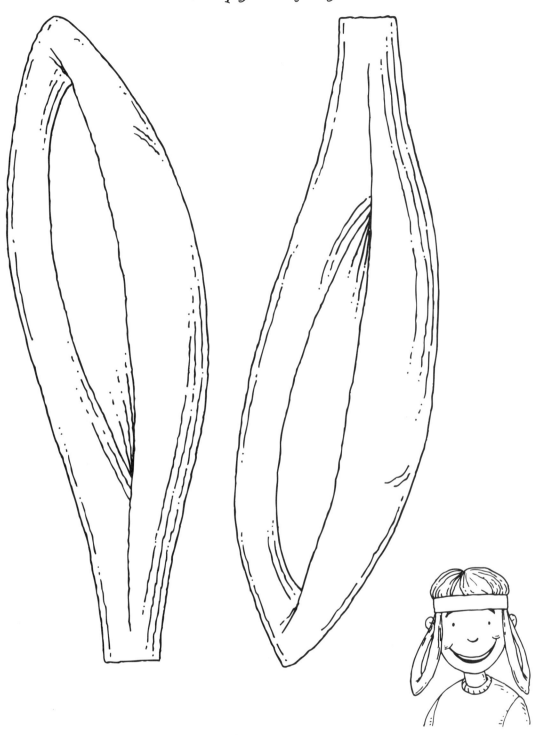

A Widow Gives All She Has

Luke 21:1-4

Jesus taught his disciples about the importance of having a truly generous heart through the seemingly insignificant gift of a poor widow. Preschoolers don't have the material means to give much to God, but they can still develop generous hearts that are pleasing to God. Help children know that it doesn't matter what they give but what's in their hearts when they give.

Clink, Clink Went the Two Little Coins

Sing this song to the tune of "Skip to My Lou." Your youngest preschoolers will love the repetitive language of this song.

Clink, clink went the coins that day *(jump up and flick your fingers away from your thumb once with each hand);*
Clink, clink went the coins that day *(repeat motion);*
Clink, clink went the coins that day *(repeat motion);*
But Jesus heard that sound. *(Cup your hand to your ear.)*

Clink, clink was all the widow had *(flick your fingers away from thumb once with each hand, then turn hands palm-up, then down);*
Clink, clink was all the widow had *(repeat motion);*
Clink, clink was all the widow had *(repeat motion);*
And she gladly gave it all. *(Stand with your hands out to your sides and spin around once.)*

Clink, clink wasn't much to give *(flick fingers away from thumb once with each hand, then shake your head);*
Clink, clink wasn't much to give *(repeat motion);*
Clink, clink wasn't much to give *(repeat motion);*
But Jesus was so pleased. *(Clap your hands on each syllable.)*

Not Small at All

Teach this action rhyme one line at a time after the children are familiar with the story.

Some people stood so tall and proud *(stretch up as tall as you can)*
When giving to the poor. *(Pretend to count out dollar bills.)*
Then Jesus saw a widow with *(make "binocular" eyes)*
A quiet, gentle heart. *(Put your hands on your heart.)*

She dropped some coins into the box *(make dropping motion with your hands),*
First one and then one more. *(Hold up one finger, then hold up a second finger.)*
Two coins were all the widow had *(hold two fingers up)*
And not a penny more. *(Shake your head.)*

Her gift was such a tiny one *(pinch your fingers together to indicate a small amount),*
'Twas almost overlooked. *(Hold your hands out to your sides.)*
But Jesus saw into her heart *(make "binocular" eyes),*
And that's why Jesus said *(wag your finger),*

"The woman there is very poor *(point to an imaginary woman),*
Yet she has given all. *(Hold your arms outstretched as far as you can.)*
And any way you look at it *(make binocular eyes),*
That's not small *(crouch down)*
At all!" *(Jump up from crouch with your arms extended.)*

Count It Out

Children will love this counting rhyme that retells the story of the widow's gift. During the counting lines, say, "three, four, five" twice as fast as you say, "one, two." Repeat the same rhythm speed for the next two lines.

One, two, *(clap once for each number),*
Three, four, five,
Six, seven,
Eight, nine, ten.
Lots of money given by lots of rich, rich men. *(Pretend to hand out money.)*

One, two *(clap on each number)*,
She put in her coins. *(Pretend to drop coins in a box.)*
She has given all she has *(extend your hands as if giving something away);*
Now she has no more. *(Hold up empty hands.)*

Many people gave their gifts *(pretend to count out bills)*,
But she gave most of all *(hold your arms out);*
For when you've given all you have
It's never *(clap)*,
Never *(clap)*
Small. *(Applaud and cheer.)*

The Gift

Use this action story to help your children see why Jesus was so pleased with the widow's gift.

A widow went to the Temple. *(Walk your fingers down your arm to rest in your palm.)*
She watched a short man count out several coins from his money pouch. *(Stroke your thumb.)*
She watched a strong man with a big money pouch give a few of his coins. *(Stroke your index finger.)*
A tall man dropped one as he put his in the box. *(Stroke your middle finger.)*
An old weak man bent down to pick up the coin and added it to his giving. *(Stroke your ring finger.)*
All she had were two little coins. *(Stroke your pinkie finger.)*
But she stood up tall and put in everything she had. *(Hold your pinkie finger up all by itself.)*
And Jesus' heart was bursting with joy *(put your hands on your heart),*
For she was the only one who gave all she had! *(Applaud!)*

The Last Supper
Matthew 26:17-30

Every child enjoys the fun of a big family meal. Eating together, whether at home or at a special restaurant, provides children with fun, food, and fellowship.

   Use these activities to help children understand Jesus' last meal with his disciples. The time Jesus spent eating with them and talking with them showed how much he loved them. Jesus' love for the children in your class is just as strong as his love for the disciples. These special activities can help you share Jesus' love with your children.

Listen Up, 'Cause Jesus Said

   Have children repeat each line as you tell the story. Let them stand and add the actions the second time through.

> **Listen up, 'cause Jesus said** *(cup your ear with your hand),*
> **"It's time to eat a meal together."** *(Pretend to set a table.)*
> **Jesus told the disciples where to find a room for the meal.**
>   *(Point.)*
> **When the disciples got there, it was just like Jesus said it**
>   **would be.** *(Walk to one side of the room, and nod and smile.)*
> **The disciples prepared the meal, and they all ate together.**
>   *(Pretend to eat.)*
>
> **Listen up, 'cause at the meal Jesus said** *(cup your ear with your*
>   *hand),*
> **"Someone in this room will turn against me."** *(Point.)*
> **The disciples were sad.** *("Paint" a frown on your face.)*

They couldn't believe that one of Jesus' friends would want to hurt him. *(Shrug your shoulders.)*

Listen up, 'cause at the meal Jesus said *(cup your ear with your hand),*
"Every time you eat this bread *(pretend to eat bread),*
You must remember that I will die for you." *(Make a cross with your fingers.)*
The disciples ate the meal and they remembered. *(Pretend to eat bread.)*

Listen up, 'cause at the meal Jesus said *(cup your ear with your hand),*
"And every time you drink this cup *(pretend to drink),*
You must remember the new promise, that when you believe in me, your sins will be forgiven." *(Pretend to wash your hands.)*
The disciples drank the cup and they remembered. *(Pretend to drink.)*

Listen up, 'cause Jesus' words were very important. *(Cup your ear with your hand.)*
The disciples remembered what he said. *(Touch your finger to your temple.)*
And the disciples wrote down what happened so that we can remember. *(Pretend to write.)*
We come to church to hear the story and we remember, too. *(Touch your finger to your temple.)*

The Last Supper

Encourage children to learn the sequence of the story of the Last Supper by playing this musical game to the tune of "Here We Go 'Round the Mulberry Bush."

This is the way they found a room *(follow a leader around the room),*
Found a room, found a room. *(Continue to follow the leader around the room. Change directions to allow different children to lead while you sing.)*
This is the way they found a room,
To share a meal with Jesus. *(Have children clap their hands on each beat.)*

This is the way they set the table *(pretend to put plates around in a circle),*
Set the table, set the table. *(Continue setting out plates.)*
This is the way they set the table
To share a meal with Jesus.

This is the way they sat and ate *(sit in a circle and pretend to eat),*
Sat and ate, sat and ate. *(Let children continue to pretend to eat.)*
This is the way they sat and ate
And shared a meal with Jesus.

This is the way he loved them so *(turn to a neighbor for a hug),*
Loved them so, loved them so. *(Continue hugging.)*
This is the way he loved them so.
It was his last supper with them.

Get Ready

Children act out the meal preparations as the story of the Last Supper is told. When the activity is complete, let children share in the meal they have prepared and talk about what they remember about Jesus.

Jesus told the disciples to prepare a room so they could share a special meal. *(Pretend to shoo the disciples away with your hand.)*
The disciples got everything ready. They set out plates. *(Set out paper plates.)*
The disciples put out cups. *(Set out paper cups.)*
The disciples put out the bread and food that they would share with Jesus during the meal. *(Help children set out simple foods like bread and fruit. Place a pitcher of fruit juice nearby.)*
When everything was ready, Jesus sat with his disciples and told God "Thank you" for the food. *(Have children bow their heads and let them take turns saying a prayer of thanks.)*
It was a happy meal because they were all together. *(Clap and cheer.)*
But it was also sad because Jesus told his friends that it would be the last meal they would have together before he died. *(Be very quiet and make a sad face.)*

Jesus gave the disciples two special ways to remember him. Jesus said when they ate the bread they could remember that he died for them. *(Pretend to eat bread.)*

And when they drank the cup they could remember the new promise that Jesus had made—that everyone's sins can be forgiven because of Jesus. *(Pretend to drink.)*

And after the meal was over, they all sang a song together. Let's sing a song, too. Then we'll enjoy our own special meal. *(Have children join in singing "Jesus Loves Me.")*

Twelve Sad Men

Through repetition and rhythm, this activity will teach about the Last Supper and help children understand that the disciples were sad to know that they wouldn't have dinner again with their Master. Have children repeat each phrase and prescribed motion.

At Passover time,
Twelve disciples got the room ready *(count to twelve quickly by touching each finger and each foot as you say each number out loud)*
And sat down to eat.

While they were eating,
Twelve disciples listened as Jesus spoke. *(Count to twelve again, but this time whisper.)*
Jesus said one of them would do something to hurt him.

Everyone looked around.
Twelve disciples wondered who he meant? *(Count to twelve with a questioning voice.)*
Who would want to hurt Jesus?

Jesus said, "Eat this bread and remember me."
Twelve disciples ate the bread and remembered Jesus. *(Count to twelve and pretend to take a bite with each number.)*
The bread helped them remember that Jesus died for them.

Jesus said, "Drink this wine and remember the promise."
Twelve disciples drank the wine and remembered. *(Count to twelve and pretend to take twelve sips.)*
The wine helped them remember that Jesus would forgive their sins.

Jesus said it was the last time he would eat with them. *(Cover your face with your hands.)*

Twelve disciples were very sad. *(Count to twelve again with a sad voice.)*

Together they sang a song and remembered Jesus. *(Sing a short praise chorus such as "Alleluia.")*

Jesus Washes the Disciples' Feet

John 13:1-17

The story of Jesus washing his disciples' feet may be a confusing one for children. Give children a little historical background before teaching this story by explaining that in Jesus' day, people wore sandals and walked everywhere. Their feet got tired, dusty, and dirty, and servants would often wash visitors' feet.

Use these activities to teach your children about the concept of service and as an introduction to Jesus' ultimate service for us.

Wiggle Toes

Young children love to take off their shoes and socks and wiggle their toes. Now you can encourage this inclination intentionally with this fun finger-and-toe play!

Have children remove their socks and shoes. Then have them form pairs and sit opposite their partners with their legs outstretched and their toes touching. Lead children in this fun finger (and toe) play. Repeat the rhyme several times so children can learn the words and actions.

Teacher Tip

If children don't want to take off their socks or shoes, that's OK. They'll enjoy the activity with their shoes on, too!

Jesus washed one follower's feet *(wiggle your toes),*

An act of service and love so sweet. *(Put your hands over your heart.)*

He took a towel and dried them, too *(pretend to dry your partner's toes);*

Then said, "You should do the same as I do." *(Shake your pointer finger.)*

Repeat the rhyme, saying two, three, four, or any number up to twelve followers. Then finish with this verse:

Jesus washed his followers' feet (*wiggle your toes*),
An act of service and love so sweet. (*Put your hands over your heart.*)
He loved them all, and he loves us, too (*hug yourself*);
So we'll serve others, 'cause he wants us to! (*Shake hands with your partner.*)

Disciple Drama

Children will love this simple drama telling how Jesus washed his followers' feet. Told from Peter's perspective, this fun drama will allow each child to experience the story. Have the children stand and repeat your words and actions.

Hi. My name is Peter. (*Point to yourself.*)
I'm one of Jesus' followers. (*Pretend to put your thumbs in imaginary suspenders.*)
We just finished eating dinner. (*Make eating motions with a pretend fork.*)
Boy! Am I ever full! (*Hold your tummy.*)
Usually after dinner, we sit around and talk (*make "talking" motions with your hands*),
And sometimes we sing a few songs. (*Pretend to direct a choir.*)
But look! Jesus is getting up from the table. (*Point in front of you.*)
I wonder what he's going to do. (*Point to your head as if wondering.*)
Hey, he's pouring water into a basin (*make a pouring motion with your hands*),
And now he's getting a towel. (*Pretend to dry your hands.*)
I can't believe it! (*Put your hands to the sides of your face in surprise.*)
He's washing everyone's feet! (*Wiggle your feet.*)
That's a job for servants—not for Jesus! (*Shake your head, and push your hands in front of you.*)
Uh-oh—now it's my turn. (*Pretend to bite your fingernails.*)
"Jesus, are you going to wash my feet?" (*Put one foot on top of the other.*)

"I can't let you, Jesus. You're my Lord!" *(Take a giant step back.)*
What's that he's saying? *(Cup your hand to your ear.)*
We should wash each other's feet? *(Point to your neighbors' feet.)*
What does he mean? *(Shrug your shoulders.)*
Oh, wait...I get it! *(Smile and point to your head.)*
Jesus was willing to serve us *(kneel, then stand up),*
And we should serve others, too! *(High five with your neighbors.)*

Willing to Wash

Children love water play. Use this simple devotion to help children learn that Jesus wants us to serve others. You'll need a basin of lukewarm water, a small bar of soap, and a thick hand towel.

Have children stand in a circle around the basin of water. (If you have a large group, form two circles around separate basins.)

Depending on the age and maturity of the children in your class, read aloud John 13:1-17 from an easy-to-understand Bible or paraphrase the story yourself.

Then say: **Jesus was willing to wash his followers' feet, even though it was a job that servants usually did. He wanted to show us that because he was willing to serve others, we should serve other people, too. Let's serve our friends here today by washing each other's hands.**

Teacher Tip

You may want to do this devotion just before snack time. That way you'll save the step of herding everyone to the sink!

Begin by gently washing the hands of the child next to you. Then use the towel to dry the child's hands. Have the child wash his or her neighbor's hands, and so on around the circle.

Then close with this prayer: **Dear Jesus, thank you for being willing to serve us. Help us to serve our friends and family. Amen.**

Serving Song

Lead children in singing this simple song to the tune of "Jesus Loves Me." Give children each a paper towel to use to act out what happens in the song.

Jesus loved his friends so true
Just as he loves me and you.

He kneeled down and washed their feet;
He showed them all a love so sweet.

Jesus served others,
Jesus served others,
Jesus served others,
To show his love so sweet.

Jesus said on bended knee:
"You should do the same as me.
Just as I have served you all,
You should mind your Master's call."

I will serve others,
I will serve others,
I will serve others,
'Cause Jesus wants me to.

Jesus Prays in the Garden

Matthew
26:36-46

Some children love to take naps. Others would claim to never nap. All of them understand what it means to fall asleep. They love to play games about going "nite-nite."

These activities will help children see that while his friends slept, Jesus prayed. The activities emphasize the need for all of us to stay awake and pray. Use these activities any time of the year to help children recognize the importance of prayer.

In the Garden Finger Play

Teach the children this finger play by saying the lines and having the children repeat them. Hold up your hand to show children the characters in the finger play.

Jesus went to the Garden one night. *(Hold up your right hand with your pointer finger up.)*

He took Peter, James, and John with him. *(Hold up your right hand with all four fingers up.)*

Jesus told them to watch and pray *(hold up your hand as a stop sign)*

While he knelt down to pray. *(Put your hands together in prayer.)*

But Peter, James, and John fell asleep. *(Hold your folded hands beside your nodding head.)*

Jesus Prayed

Lead children in singing the following song to the tune of "Frère Jacques." Tell children to repeat your words as you sing. Encourage children to do the motions in the parentheses.

In the Garden (*spread your hands*)
Jesus prayed. (*Fold your hands in prayer.*)
"Peter, James, and John (*touch each of your first three fingers as
each name is sung*),
Please pray with me." (*Fold your hands in prayer.*)

In the Garden (*spread your hands*)
Jesus prayed. (*Fold your hands.*)
But Peter, James, and John (*touch each of your first three fingers
as each name is sung*)
Fell asleep. (*Put your hands under your head to show sleep.*)

Peter, James, and John

Children will love this simple guessing game that helps to tell the story of Jesus' prayer time in the Garden. One child sits in the middle of the circle and "prays" while three other children are chosen to be "Peter," "James," and "John." They all three make yawning noises. The child in the center guesses who is yawning. Use a blindfold, or have the child in the middle cover his or her eyes.

If you have fewer than six children, have one child play the roles of Peter, James, and John.

Have children sit in a circle. Have a volunteer sit in the middle. Instruct the child in the middle to close his or her eyes and to bow his or her head as you say the following:

Jesus went to the Garden to pray. (*Have the child in the middle
bow his or her head and close his or her eyes.*)
He took three friends with him. (*Walk around the circle.*)
He took Peter. (*Tap one child, and have him or her yawn.*)
He took James. (*Tap another child, and have him or her yawn.*)
He took John. (*Tap a third child, and have him or her yawn.*)
When Jesus came back, they were all sleeping. (*Have the child
in the middle open his or her eyes and try to guess who the three
sleepyheads are.*)

Continue playing until each child who wants a turn in the middle has a chance to try.

In the Garden

Lead children in this movement-oriented activity to help them understand what happened the night Jesus prayed in the Garden.

Help children form two groups. Explain that one group will follow the actions of Jesus in the story while the other group will do what the three disciples did that night. Let groups change roles and act out the story a second time to allow both groups a chance to play both roles.

This activity works best if each group has a teen or adult helper to help kids do the actions while you read the text.

> **One night, Jesus was very sad, so he went to the Garden to pray.** *(Have Group One walk toward the middle of the room.)*
>
> **Peter, James, and John went with Jesus.** *(Have Group Two follow Group One.)*
>
> **Jesus asked the three to wait for him while he prayed.** *(Group One should walk to a corner of the room and kneel down as if praying.)*
>
> **Peter, James, and John waited, but soon they fell asleep.** *(Group Two should stay in the middle of the room as they lie down and pretend to sleep.)*
>
> **Jesus came back and said: "Can't you stay awake for even one hour? Please watch and pray."** *(Have Group One come back to the middle of the room and pretend to talk to Group Two. Have Group Two pretend to wake up.)*
>
> **Jesus went away again to pray.** *(Group One should return to the same corner and kneel again in prayer.)*
>
> **The three disciples fell asleep again.** *(Group Two should lie down.)*
>
> **When Jesus came back again** *(Group One should walk back to the middle),*
>
> **He found the three sleeping again. But this time, Jesus didn't wake them up.** *(Have Group One shake their heads but not wake Group Two up. Group One should turn and go back to the corner again.)*
>
> **Jesus went back again to pray without waking his friends.**
>
> **When Jesus came back, he woke them up and said, "Are you still sleeping?"** *(Have Group One go back and "wake" the sleeping disciples.)*
>
> **Jesus' friends just couldn't stay awake.**

Jesus Dies

Matthew 26:47–27:66

Some young children may not have encountered death yet. Others may have experienced the loss of a pet or close relative. But regardless of their experiences, you can be sure that preschoolers don't understand what death is.

To make this part of Jesus' life easier for preschoolers to understand, use these activities to focus on Jesus' love for us and his sacrifice. Explain that God sent Jesus to die on the cross so that everyone could receive forgiveness and become God's friend. Use these activities to help children understand that Jesus died on the cross because he loves them.

As you're doing these activities, be especially sensitive to those who may feel sad or upset by this lesson. Offer these children comfort, and explain that Jesus is alive today.

Easter Drama

Kids will enjoy acting out the Easter story with this active drama. Each child acts out the entire story. Have the children stand and repeat your words and actions. Clear a large area in the middle of the room to allow the children to move around.

Jesus walked and talked with men. *(Have children walk around pretending to talk to each other.)*

He had a lot of friends. *(Have children shake hands with each other.)*

But one sad day the soldiers came *(have children stomp their feet)*

And took our Lord away. *(Grab one wrist and pull it in front of you.)*

They took him to the leading men *(have children all walk to one corner of the room)*
And to a man in charge. *(Have children walk to another corner.)*
Jesus didn't say a word. *(Cover your mouth.)*
He was quiet as a lamb. *(Make a hushing sound.)*
The people wanted him to die *(shake your fist)*
Though he'd done nothing wrong. *(Shake your head sadly.)*
So Jesus carried his cross to a hill. *(Pretend to carry a heavy cross and move to another corner of the room.)*
It was so sad to see. *(Rub your eyes as if crying.)*
Then Jesus prayed for all the people. *(Bow your head.)*
He loved them all so much. *(Stretch out your arms.)*
Jesus died on the cross that day *(stretch out your arms)*
To save us all from sin. *(Hug yourself.)*
But Jesus' story doesn't end there! *(Hold up one finger.)*
Jesus rose from the dead. *(Jump up.)*
He's alive! *(Cheer.)*

Jesus Loves Me

Lead children in singing this song to the tune of "This Old Man." Encourage them to do the motions with you.

Jesus died
On the cross *(stretch your arms out in a cross shape)*
To save a world that was lost. *(Make a circular motion using both hands.)*
He died to show his love for you and me *(place your hands over your heart)*
And from sin to set us free! *(Hold your hands up high over your head.)*

Jesus Died

This fun activity shows both the sorrow we feel for Jesus' death and the elation we feel because of his resurrection. At the end of the story, build the excitement in your children by starting off the chant softly. Each time you repeat the chant, say the second line louder and louder until the children are cheering loudly. Sit in a circle to begin.

One night Jesus was praying in the Garden *(fold your hands)*,
Then soldiers came and arrested him. *(Make fists and tap your wrists together.)*
All of Jesus' friends were scared, and they ran away. *(Pump your arms in a running motion.)*
Jesus was all alone. *(Hold up one finger.)*
Jesus was arrested because some people thought he did bad things. *(Wag your finger.)*
But Jesus never did anything wrong. *(Shake your head.)*
The people were so sure that Jesus did bad things that they killed him. *(Rub your eyes as if crying.)*
Jesus died, but three days later he came back to life. *(Tap three fingers, then clap.)*
No one but Jesus can come back to life again. *(Point up.)*
Yea! Jesus! *(Clap.)*

The Chant:
Jesus died—Boo, hoo, hoo. *(Rub your eyes as if crying.)*
But now he lives—Yeah! Yeah! Yeah! *(Wave your arms above your head.)*

God's Friend

This activity will help children realize that Jesus' death and resurrection have given us a way to "make friends" with God.

You'll need a "Jesus" pillow for this activity. Draw a large picture of Jesus on an old solid-color pillowcase. To make this easy, photocopy a picture of Jesus onto an overhead projector transparency. Then use an overhead projector to shine the picture of Jesus onto the wall. Trace the picture onto the pillowcase and then color it. You can use fabric markers or even watercolor markers. Then put a pillow into the pillowcase.

Have the children sit in a circle. Put the Jesus pillow on your lap. Say: **We know that Jesus was kind and loving. He helped people who were sick and sad. But not everyone knew the truth about Jesus. Some people thought Jesus was a bad man. They arrested him and killed him. Jesus died to take away our sins. But after three days, Jesus rose from the dead. Today Jesus is alive. And we can be friends with him. Let's show Jesus how much we love him. Jesus lives in heaven, but we'll pretend that this pillow is Jesus.**

Pass the pillow around the room, and have the children hug the pillow. Encourage them to treat the pillow nicely as if it really were Jesus. As the pillow comes to each child, say: (Child's name), **you can be Jesus' friend. Jesus loves you.** Some children may want to say something to Jesus. Encourage them to say "I love you" or "I want to be your friend, too."

Jesus Lives

Matthew 28:1-10

Young children may not understand everything about Jesus' death and resurrection, but they'll enjoy celebrating that Jesus is alive. And they can also understand that Jesus wants to be their friend and that he is always there to help us.

Use these activities to build the children's excitement in the resurrected Christ. Let children enjoy the celebration and joy of his appearances to his friends. These activities should allow children an opportunity to express joy and excitement. Share them at any time during the year to remind children that Jesus is alive!

Resurrection Drama

Have children act out the Easter story as they follow your directions for motion and sound effects.

Jesus died and was put in a grave. *(Squat down and curl into a little ball.)*

A giant rock was rolled in front of the place. *(Pound on the floor with your hands.)*

His friends cried and were sad that he was dead. *(Pretend to cry.)*

But on the third day, something happened. *(Count to three on your fingers.)*

A giant earthquake rocked the ground. *(Have children stomp their feet and clap.)*

The giant stone rolled away. *(Have children roll over on the floor.)*

Mary and her friends walked to the grave. *(Walk in place.)*

They felt the earthquake. *(Stomp your feet.)*

They ran to the open grave. *(Run in place.)*
They looked in. *(Cup your hand over your eyes.)*
A bright angel was inside the grave. *(Shield your eyes from the brightness.)*
The women were sad and afraid. *(Act scared.)*
The angel told the women that Jesus was alive! *(Cheer.)*
And so the women went to tell the disciples. *(Run in place.)*
Jesus appeared to them. *(Act surprised.)*
The women fell down at his feet. *(Fall to the floor.)*
They were so happy to see him! *(Cheer and hug each other.)*

Easter Puppets

Kids will love telling the Easter story over and over again with the help of these simple finger puppets. You'll need three-by-three-inch squares of scrap fabric, masking tape, and washable markers. For each child, make two woman puppets from patterned fabric, an angel puppet from white or golden fabric, and a Jesus puppet from red or purple fabric.

To make a puppet, place the material over a child's finger, secure it at the middle with masking tape to fit the width of the child's finger, and draw a simple face on it at the fingertip. Make sure the puppets fit snugly yet are able to be easily removed and replaced.

Have children begin the puppet play with all four puppets in front of them on the floor.

Jesus died and was put in a grave. *(Put the Jesus puppet beside you on the floor.)*
His friends were very sad. *(Put the two women puppets on your right hand and then fold your fingers down to make them look sad.)*
When the women went to where Jesus was buried ("walk" your right hand toward where Jesus is),
An earthquake shook the ground. *(Bounce your right hand up and down.)*
Then an angel met them there. *(Put the angel puppet on your left hand.)*

The angel told the women that Jesus was alive. *(Have the angel puppet "talk" to the women.)*

The women were very happy and started to run to tell Jesus' friends. *(Move your right hand quickly away from your left hand.)*

But before they could run, Jesus was there with them. *(Put the Jesus puppet on your left hand.)*

Jesus said, "Greetings." *(Wiggle the Jesus puppet.)*

The women fell down at Jesus' feet. *(Put the women puppets down at the bottom of the Jesus puppet.)*

They were happy to see Jesus again! *(Have the puppets all "hug.")*

Go and Tell

Help children learn to share their faith with this fun mingling activity. Have children stand in a circle and complete the actions with the children standing next to them.

Go tell a friend *(have children repeat the phrase)*
That Jesus was buried in a grave. *(Have children repeat.)*
Now go tell everyone while you sadly pat a back. *(Encourage each child to turn to the child next to him or her, gently pat his or her back, and repeat the phrase "Jesus was buried in a grave.")*

Go tell a friend. *(Have children repeat the phrase.)*
Jesus was dead for three days. *(Have children repeat.)*
Now go tell everyone as you count to three. *(Encourage each child to turn to the child next to him or her, count to three, and repeat the phrase "Jesus was dead for three days.")*

Go tell a friend. *(Have children repeat the phrase.)*
The sad women went to the grave. *(Repeat.)*
Now go tell everyone as you hug and cry. *(Encourage each child to hug the child next to him or her and pretend to cry as he or she repeats the phrase "The sad women went to the grave.")*

Go tell a friend. *(Repeat.)*
There was a giant earthquake. *(Repeat.)*
Now go tell everyone as you tremble and shake. *(Encourage children to move around and shake as they repeat the phrase "There was a giant earthquake.")*

Go tell a friend *(repeat)*
That an angel met the women. *(Repeat.)*
Now go tell everyone as you cover your eyes from the brightness of the angel. *(Encourage each child to turn to the*

child next to him or her and say, "An angel met the women" as he or she covers his or her eyes.)

Go tell a friend *(repeat)*
That Jesus is alive! *(Repeat.)*
Now go tell everyone as you pass out hugs of happiness! *(Encourage children to share hugs with the children next to them as they repeat the phrase "Jesus is alive!")*

Now We See You

Children will enjoy hiding and popping out to surprise their friends. This active game will help children understand the excitement Jesus' disciples felt when they saw him alive again. Encourage children to follow your directions to play the game. Continue playing until each child has hidden and popped out.

After Jesus died on the cross, he was buried. *(Hold up a blanket.)*
No one could see him. *(Cover someone with the blanket.)*
He was buried for three days. *(Lead children in counting out loud "one, two, three!")*
Then Jesus was alive again *(have the blanketed child jump up and throw off the blanket),*
And his disciples were so happy! *(Have everyone jump around until you hold the blanket up for the next child to take a turn.)*
And we can be happy too, because Jesus is still alive!

Jesus Goes to Heaven

Mark
16:15-16,
19-20

Young children know how it feels to say goodbye to someone they love. Sometimes having a parent leave the Sunday school classroom can be traumatic. Helping children understand about Jesus leaving earth to return to heaven can be confusing.

Use these activities to help children realize that even though we can't see Jesus, his Spirit is still here with us. Throughout the year, these activities will reinforce Jesus' constant presence and love.

Jesus Is Alive!

This active story takes children through Jesus' death, resurrection, and ascension. Begin this story with everyone sitting on the floor in a circle.

Jesus died upon the cross. (*Rub your eyes as if crying.*)

He was buried in a grave. (*Bow your head.*)

For three sad days, our Lord was dead (*count to three*),

But then came Sunday morning. (*Rest one forearm on top of the other. Raise the top forearm to show the sun rising.*)

When the women came to see (*have children stand up while holding hands*),

An earthquake shook the ground. (*Lean from side to side in circle while continuing to hold hands.*)

Jesus' body was not there. (*Hang your head in sadness.*)

He'd risen from the dead! (*Jump up and cheer.*)

He talked and walked with all his friends. (*Walk around and shake hands.*)

He said: "Go tell the world. (*Move your hands as if they were mouths.*)

If the people will believe in me *(spread your hands to indicate all the people),*
They'll be my forever friends." *(Hug yourself.)*
Then Jesus went up, up, up into heaven *(stand on tiptoe and then jump up),*
And we have a job to do. *(Have each child tell the child next to him or her that Jesus is alive.)*

Go to the World

Let children enjoy the run and fun of this game as they learn to share the Good News. Play this in an open area outside or in a large room with the furniture cleared away. You'll need colorful rolls of crepe paper so that each child can have a one-foot strip.

Give each child a one-foot strip of crepe paper. Have the children scatter around the room. On "go," encourage each child to run to a friend and give the crepe paper to him or her. When children give away their paper, have them say, "Jesus rose from the dead!" When they receive a piece of crepe paper from someone, have them say, "I believe."

When everyone has traded crepe paper at least once, clap your hands to signal the next part of the game. When you clap, tell children to throw their crepe paper pieces in the air and say, "Jesus went up into heaven." Then encourage children to pick up their crepe paper to start again. The second time, have children say, "Jesus is still with us" as they give away a piece of crepe paper and "Tell the world" as they receive a piece.

Good News

Help children get excited about sharing God with the world as they enjoy spreading the news around the church. Lead children in this march during a fellowship time or an open time in the Sunday school or church service. Say each phrase and then have the children repeat it and do the actions.

Jesus said to go and tell. *(Have children repeat the phrase as they pump their arms at their sides.)*
So we want to share the Good News. *(Hold your hands out toward the people.)*
Jesus died and rose again *(stretch your arms out to your sides, then above your head),*

Then he went up to heaven. *(Have children jump up.)*
Now we want to tell the whole world. *(Spin around once on the word "world.")*
Jesus is alive! *(Cheer.)*

We Will Go

Kids will love this active way to understand God's call for all to go and tell the world.

Have children begin this activity sitting in a small circle in the middle of the room.

After Jesus rose from the dead,
He met with his disciples. *(Spread your hands to indicate the children.)*
"Go to all the world," Jesus said *(encourage children to run to the farthest point from where they were sitting),*
And share the Good News." So what would you tell someone about Jesus? *(Let children take turns sharing what they know about Jesus.)*
Then Jesus said that anyone who believes the Good News will live with Jesus forever. *(Have the children spread their arms wide and run back to the small circle again.)*
After Jesus said that, he went up and up and up. *(Show children how to rise up slowly, a little bit more with each "up," until they are standing on their tiptoes.)*
Jesus went up into heaven,
And he gave his friends a job to do.
They were to go and tell the whole world that Jesus had risen from the dead,
And so they did! *(Have children run back to the far edges of the room.)*

Group Publishing, Inc.
Attention: Books & Curriculum
P.O. Box 481
Loveland, CO 80539
Fax: (970) 669-1994

Evaluation for Wiggly, Giggly Bible Stories About Jesus

Please help Group Publishing, Inc., continue to provide innovative and useful resources for ministry. Please take a moment to fill out this evaluation and mail or fax it to us. Thanks!

• • •

1. As a whole, this book has been (circle one)

not very helpful   very helpful

1   2   3   4   5   6   7   8   9   10

2. The best things about this book:

3. Ways this book could be improved:

4. Things I will change because of this book:

5. Other books I'd like to see Group publish in the future:

6. Would you be interested in field-testing future Group products and giving us your feedback? If so, please fill in the information below:

Name _____

Street Address _____

City_____ State _____ Zip _____

Phone Number _____ Date _____

TEACH YOUR PRESCHOOLERS AS JESUS TAUGHT WITH GROUP'S *HANDS-ON BIBLE CURRICULUM*™

Hands-On Bible Curriculum™ **for preschoolers** helps your preschoolers learn the way they learn best—by touching, exploring, and discovering. With active learning, preschoolers love learning about the Bible, and they really remember what they learn.

Because small children learn best through repetition, Preschoolers and Pre-K & K will learn one important point per lesson, and Toddlers & 2s will learn one point each month with **Hands-On Bible Curriculum**. These important lessons will stick with them and comfort them during their daily lives. Your children will learn:

- •God is our friend,
- •who Jesus is, and
- •we can always trust Jesus.

The **Learning Lab®** is packed with age-appropriate learning tools for fun, faith-building lessons. Toddlers & 2s explore big **Interactive StoryBoards**™ with enticing textures that toddlers love to touch—like sandpaper for earth, cotton for clouds, and blue cellophane for water. While they hear the Bible story, children also *touch* the Bible story. And they learn. **Bible Big Books**™ captivate Preschoolers and Pre-K & K while teaching them important Bible lessons. With **Jumbo Bible Puzzles**™ and involving **Learning Mats**™, your children will see, touch, and explore their Bible stories. Each quarter there's a brand new collection of supplies to keep your lessons fresh and involving.

Fuzzy, age-appropriate hand puppets are also available to add to the learning experience. What better way to teach your class than with the help of an attention-getting teaching assistant? These child-friendly puppets help you teach each lesson with scripts provided in the **Teacher Guide**. Plus, your children will enjoy teaching the puppets what they learn. Cuddles the Lamb, Whiskers the Mouse, and Pockets the Kangaroo turn each lesson into an interactive and entertaining learning experience.

Just order one **Learning Lab** and one **Teacher Guide** for each age level, add a few common classroom supplies, and presto—you have everything you need to inspire and build faith in your children. For more interactive fun, introduce your children to the age-appropriate puppet who will be your teaching assistant and their friend. No student books are required!

Hands-On Bible Curriculum is also available for elementary grades.

Active-Learning Resources for Your Children's Ministry

Incredible Edible Bible Fun

More than 50 kid-friendly and teacher-approved recipes make learning fun *and* tasty! Each recipe ties to a simple, age-appropriate devotion. And children will stir up their creations safely and quickly—no sharp knives, hot ovens, or refrigerators are needed, and each recipe takes just 20 minutes from start to finish. Deep, memorable Bible learning has never tasted so good!   ISBN 0-7644-2001-1

Fun & Easy Easter Pageant: Life Savers
Paul N. Lessard

Now children's drama success is guaranteed—with this fully prepared pageant that makes Easter planning simple. Children simply pantomime parts—voices, music, and sound effects are on the included compact disc! The fun setting—an Animal Awards Night—makes it easy to perform this drama on a stage...in a classroom... even outside! And audiences join in the fun by singing new Easter celebration lyrics to familiar melodies. Any church with a children's ministry or puppet ministry (puppets can play these parts too!) will enjoy this easily prepared, fun-to-perform drama. And it's not just for Easter—the message is timeless, and so are the smiles kids will see on the faces of their audiences.   ISBN 1-55945-499-7

The Children's Worker's Encyclopedia of Bible-Teaching Ideas

New ideas—and lots of them!—for captivating children with stories from the Bible. Children's workers get over 350 attention-grabbing, active-learning devotions...art and craft projects...creative prayers...service projects...field trips...music suggestions...quiet reflection activities...skits...and more—winning ideas from each and every book of the Bible! Simple, step-by-step directions make it easy to slide an idea into any meeting— on short notice—with little or no preparation. BONUS: It's easy to find exactly the right idea on a moment's notice! Handy indexes outline ideas by Scripture, theme, and idea style.

Old Testament   ISBN 1-55945-622-1
New Testament   ISBN 1-55945-625-6

Helping Children Live Like Jesus

Before children can love Jesus they must *know* him—and these 13 lessons help Sunday school and Bible club leaders introduce Jesus in a fun, active-learning way that reaches any learning style. Crafts, skits, art projects, interactive stories, object lessons, and guided group discussions—they're all here. And every activity draws children back to the "good news," a Bible-based focus for each lesson. Children will examine the life of Jesus from birth to his resurrection. Included: lesson outlines, preparation guide, and a BONUS: photocopiable handouts that help teachers reinforce Bible lessons!   ISBN 1-55945-681-7

More Active-Learning Resources for Your Children's Ministry

Group's Brite-Tite™ Can o' Fun
Glenn Q. Bannerman, Beth B. Gunn & Lee Ann B. Konopka
Here's the quick and easy way to create soft, safe, funtastic games to play at church…
school…camp…parties…and home! You'll easily turn colorful nylon tubes into
rackets…rag balls…doughnuts…flying disks…all to be used for extra-fun activities. Plus,
you get step-by-step instructions for making…
- non-competitive events…
- creative crafts…
- fast-action activities…and
- graceful movement exercises for children, youth, and adults.

For indoor play…outside fun…Brite-Tites™ make every game time easy—and every day
a celebration! Comes with Brite-Tites in a variety of colors.   ISBN 1-55945-626-4

Group's Brite-Tite™ Book o' Fun   ISBN 1-55945-497-0

Bunch o' Brite-Tites™ (bag of 44)   ISBN 1-55945-771-6

Party! Party! for Children's Ministry
Susan L. Lingo
Now planning parties for your children is easy—and every party will come off without a
glitch! Here are complete plans for over a dozen exciting, affordable events guaranteed
to be as much fun for *you* as they are for your children! You'll get: unique new crafts…
games your kids have never played before…icebreakers sure to put every child in the
"party mood"…as well as reproducible planning checklists, invitations, fliers, and press
releases. Plus you get timesaving tips, decorating plans, and a list of party suppliers!

Use these easy-to-organize parties to help your children build friendships…make visitors
feel welcome…and celebrate your children's successes! Order today!   ISBN 1-55945-609-4

Eye-Popping 3-D Bulletin Boards
Susan L. Lingo
Get 24 ready-to-go ideas *guaranteed* to involve your children in creating and learning
from fun bulletin boards! With Group's **Eye-Popping 3-D Bulletin Boards,** you'll get…
- **25 Dynamite Displays**—reinforcing Bible truths…celebrating holidays…and
  encouraging children to play and pray!
- **36 Quick-Make Patterns**—so you can quickly and easily create pop-up cards…
  angels…folding lions and lambs…disciples…and more!
- **Tricks of the Trade**—practical techniques and tools that make it easy to design your
  own bulletin boards, door displays, sensational ceilings, table-toppers, and more!

Now you can make the best possible use of bulletin boards—so your kids learn even
more about Jesus and the Bible!   ISBN 1-55945-904-2

Order today from your local Christian bookstore, or write:
Group Publishing, P.O. Box 485, Loveland, CO 80539.